OPPOSING
VIEWPOINTS®
SERIES

Trumpism and the Future of the Republican Party

Other Books of Related Interest

Opposing Viewpoints Series

America's Changing Demographics
Campaign Finance
The Fifth Estate: Extreme Viewpoints from Alternative Media
Identity Politics
Party Politics
Politics and Journalism in a Post-Truth World

At Issue Series

Celebrities in Politics
Gerrymandering and Voting Districts
Partisanship
Political Corruption
Politicians on Social Media
The Politicization of the Supreme Court

Current Controversies Series

Are There Two Americas?
Attacks on Science
The Capitol Riot: Fragile Democracy
Hate Groups
Political Extremism in the United States
The Two-Party System in the United States

> "Congress shall make no law ... abridging the freedom of speech, or of the press."

First Amendment to the US Constitution

The basic foundation of our democracy is the First Amendment guarantee of freedom of expression. The Opposing Viewpoints series is dedicated to the concept of this basic freedom and the idea that it is more important to practice it than to enshrine it.

OPPOSING
VIEWPOINTS®
SERIES

Trumpism and the Future of the Republican Party

Gary Wiener, Book Editor

GREENHAVEN
PUBLISHING

Published in 2022 by Greenhaven Publishing, LLC
353 3rd Avenue, Suite 255, New York, NY 10010

Copyright © 2022 by Greenhaven Publishing, LLC

First Edition

Articles in Greenhaven Publishing anthologies are often edited for length to meet page
requirements. In addition, original titles of these works are changed to clearly present
the main thesis and to explicitly indicate the author's opinion. Every effort is made to
ensure that Greenhaven Publishing accurately reflects the original intent of the authors.
Every effort has been made to trace the owners of the copyrighted material.

Cover image: George Sheldon/Shutterstock.com

Library of Congress CataloginginPublication Data

Names: Wiener, Gary, editor.
Title: Trumpism and the future of the republican party / Gary Wiener.
Description: First edition. | New York : Greenhaven Publishing, 2022. |
   Series: Opposing viewpoints | Includes bibliographical references and
   index. | Contents: Trumpism and the future of the republica | Audience:
   Ages 15+ | Audience: Grades 10-12 | Summary: "Anthology of curated
   essays exploring Donald Trump's role as leader of the Republican party
   and what will happen to the party beyond his presidency"-- Provided by
   publisher.
Identifiers: LCCN 2021035613 | ISBN 9781534508378 (library binding) | ISBN
   9781534508361 (paperback)
Subjects: LCSH: Republican Party (U.S. : 1854-)--History--Juvenile
   literature. | Trump, Donald, 1946---Influence--Juvenile literature. |
   United States--Politics and government--2017---Juvenile literature.
Classification: LCC JK2356 .T79 2022 | DDC 324.2734--dc23
LC record available at https://lccn.loc.gov/2021035613

Manufactured in the United States of America

Website: http://greenhavenpublishing.com

Contents

The Importance of Opposing Viewpoints

Perhaps every generation experiences a period in time in which the populace seems especially polarized, starkly divided on the important issues of the day and gravitating toward the far ends of the political spectrum and away from a consensus-facilitating middle ground. The world that today's students are growing up in and that they will soon enter into as active and engaged citizens is deeply fragmented in just this way. Issues relating to terrorism, immigration, women's rights, minority rights, race relations, health care, taxation, wealth and poverty, the environment, policing, military intervention, the proper role of government—in some ways, perennial issues that are freshly and uniquely urgent and vital with each new generation—are currently roiling the world.

If we are to foster a knowledgeable, responsible, active, and engaged citizenry among today's youth, we must provide them with the intellectual, interpretive, and critical-thinking tools and experience necessary to make sense of the world around them and of the all-important debates and arguments that inform it. After all, the outcome of these debates will in large measure determine the future course, prospects, and outcomes of the world and its peoples, particularly its youth. If they are to become successful members of society and productive and informed citizens, students need to learn how to evaluate the strengths and weaknesses of someone else's arguments, how to sift fact from opinion and fallacy, and how to test the relative merits and validity of their own opinions against the known facts and the best possible available information. The landmark series OpposingViewpoints has been providing students with just such critical-thinking skills and exposure to the debates surrounding society's most urgent contemporary issues for many years, and it continues to serve this essential role with undiminished commitment, care, and rigor.

The key to the series's success in achieving its goal of sharpening students' critical-thinking and analytic skills resides in its title—

Opposing Viewpoints. In every intriguing, compelling, and engaging volume of this series, readers are presented with the widest possible spectrum of distinct viewpoints, expert opinions, and informed argumentation and commentary, supplied by some of today's leading academics, thinkers, analysts, politicians, policy makers, economists, activists, change agents, and advocates. Every opinion and argument anthologized here is presented objectively and accorded respect. There is no editorializing in any introductory text or in the arrangement and order of the pieces. No piece is included as a "straw man," an easy ideological target for cheap point-scoring. As wide and inclusive a range of viewpoints as possible is offered, with no privileging of one particular political ideology or cultural perspective over another. It is left to each individual reader to evaluate the relative merits of each argument— as he or she sees it, and with the use of ever-growing critical-thinking skills—and grapple with his or her own assumptions, beliefs, and perspectives to determine how convincing or successful any given argument is and how the reader's own stance on the issue may be modified or altered in response to it.

This process is facilitated and supported by volume, chapter, and selection introductions that provide readers with the essential context they need to begin engaging with the spotlighted issues, with the debates surrounding them, and with their own perhaps shifting or nascent opinions on them. In addition, guided reading and discussion questions encourage readers to determine the authors' point of view and purpose, interrogate and analyze the various arguments and their rhetoric and structure, evaluate the arguments' strengths and weaknesses, test their claims against available facts and evidence, judge the validity of the reasoning, and bring into clearer, sharper focus the reader's own beliefs and conclusions and how they may differ from or align with those in the collection or those of their classmates.

Research has shown that reading comprehension skills improve dramatically when students are provided with compelling, intriguing, and relevant "discussable" texts. The subject matter of these collections could not be more compelling, intriguing, or urgently relevant to today's students and the world they are poised to inherit. The anthologized articles and the reading and discussion questions that are included with them also provide the basis for stimulating, lively, and passionate classroom debates. Students who are compelled to anticipate objections to their own argument and identify the flaws in those of an opponent read more carefully, think more critically, and steep themselves in relevant context, facts, and information more thoroughly. In short, using discussable text of the kind provided by every single volume in the Opposing Viewpointsseries encourages close reading, facilitates reading comprehension, fosters research, strengthens critical thinking, and greatly enlivens and energizes classroom discussion and participation. The entire learning process is deepened, extended, and strengthened.

For all of these reasons, Opposing Viewpointscontinues to be exactly the right resource at exactly the right time—when we most need to provide readers with the critical-thinking tools and skills that will not only serve them well in school but also in their careers and their daily lives as decision-making family members, community members, and citizens. This series encourages respectful engagement with and analysis of opposing viewpoints and fosters a resulting increase in the strength and rigor of one's own opinions and stances. As such, it helps make readers "future ready," and that readiness will pay rich dividends for the readers themselves, for the citizenry, for our society, and for the world at large.

Introduction

"Watching the Republican Party is like watching a friend drink himself to death. There's a mix of sadness and anger tinged by a bit of sympathy for the misery he tries to hide. But alcoholism is a disease and political cowardice is just what it looks like: weakness and opportunism mixed with fear and self-loathing."

—Republican strategist Stuart Stevens

D onald Trump's 2016 presidential election victory was a surprise. Hillary Clinton, his opponent, was favored by a wide margin and Trump himself was planning for life after a failed presidential run. He was reportedly shocked when he won.

The victory was historic in many ways. First, Trump received almost three million fewer votes than his opponent but prevailed convincingly in the electoral college. Second, he was a president with no prior experience running a government on any level. And third, no chief executive in modern history has turned government—and party politics—upside down as thoroughly as has President Donald John Trump.

It soon became clear that "Trumpism," the name given to the philosophy by which he governed, stood firmly for a number of key objectives. Trump would put America first, by protecting economic interests both at home and abroad. He would harness the xenophobia, or fear of foreigners, which was a core policy of contemporary conservatism, by limiting immigration and cutting refugees. He would also alienate key US allies such as Germany's Angela Merkel while cozying up to strongmen, including Russia's Vladimir Putin, Korea's Kim Jong-un, and Turkey's Recep Erdoğan. And he would offer enormous tax cuts, the bulk of which would benefit corporations and the very rich.

These policies were embraced by most conservatives and loathed by liberals. But it was Trump's numerous attacks on America's underclass, either by words or enacted policies, that really turned off many in the United States, including a group of traditional Republicans who had never warmed to him. He called Mexican immigrants criminals and rapists; he seemed to coddle hate groups such as those who marched in Charlottesville, Virginia.

Trump had won the presidency despite alienating many of the traditional Republican politicians who had guided the party for years. The so-called never Trumpers fled from the brash and bullying candidate. Among the old guard Republicans who initially opposed Trump were Jeb Bush, Ted Cruz, Lindsay Graham, Carly Fiorina, John Kasich, and Colin Powell. Yet Trump had the ear of many average Americans—and still does today. Some of those who had opposed him, such as Cruz and Graham, came crawling back after his victory and have remained loyal after his subsequent defeat.

Trump reigned over America for a tempestuous four years, but it was after he lost the 2020 election by seven million raw votes and seventy-four electoral college votes that the fireworks really began. He insisted that the election was fraudulent and that he had won by a wide margin. He demanded recounts, to which he was entitled, but the vote did not change appreciably. He launched more than sixty lawsuits challenging the election count, but he lost nearly every one of them. He attempted to cajole, harass, and badger state Republican leaders into altering the vote in his favor.

Former president Obama had this to say about Trump's machinations: "What we saw was my successor … violate that core tenet that you count the votes and then declare a winner— and fabricate and make up a whole bunch of hooey." Trump's usually loyal-to-a-fault attorney general phrased it less politely.

"It was all bullsh*t," Bill Barr said of his boss's campaign to alter the election results.

It was Trump's final and most shocking move, allegedly instigating the Capitol riot of January 6, 2021, that really sliced his party into two groups, those who would follow him anywhere, and those ready to jump ship.

No one personifies the Republican Party schism more than Liz Cheney, daughter of Republican Vice-President (to George W. Bush) Dick Cheney, and Congresswoman from Wyoming. Before the Capitol insurrection, Liz Cheney was an esteemed member of the party, having risen in Congress to the rank of chair of the House Republican Conference, the third-highest position in the House Republican leadership, a post she held from 2019 to 2021. She was a Trump loyalist who had voted with him over 92 percent of the time.

But for Cheney, the Capitol riot was the breaking point. She was appalled by Trump's actions, and she said so in no uncertain terms. She was not alone. Senate Minority Leader Mitch McConnell and House Minority Leader Kevin McCarthy had displayed similar reactions. But in the end, many like McConnell and McCarthy retreated to the Trump camp. Cheney did not. On January 13, 2021, she was one of ten Republicans in the House of Representatives who voted to impeach Donald Trump.

As a result, the House, led by McCarthy, held a vote designed to strip Cheney of her leadership position. House Republicans overwhelmingly chose Trump over truth, and Cheney was demoted. She does not regret her choice to impeach the former president, however. "This is about being able to tell your kids that you stood up and did the right thing," she said.

Trump, for his part, vowed to get rid of "the Liz Cheneys of the world." Nothing is more important to the former president than loyalty, and Republicans such as Cheney and the nine others who voted against him in the House became targets of Trump's revenge.

Such a scenario presages the future of the Republican Party. It is no longer just the country that is divided. Now, Republicans themselves are split into two factions, pro- and anti-Trump. But it is clear which side is winning. Cheney's demotion was just one indicator. During that January 6th joint session of Congress to certify the election, more than 100 Republican House members, including leader Kevin McCarthy, voted against certifying election results in Arizona and Pennsylvania, despite having no proof of widespread voter fraud. These elected officials were still firmly beholden to Donald Trump, and no amount of evidence was going to shake their commitment to their leader.

Republican efforts to undermine democracy accelerated after the 2020 election. States such as Georgia and Texas have enacted stricter voting policies that seemingly target minorities. Arizona Republicans hired a partisan firm to audit the November 2020 election in a non-binding bid to overturn the results. And Trump fans continue to turn up to his rallies, convinced that he is still president. "I know he won," one woman wearing a "TRUMP WON" shirt told Buzzfeed news at a June 2021 Trump rally in Ohio. "There's so much evidence out there it was stolen," she said. "Jesus Christ would have to come down and tell me that Biden won before I would ever believe it."

In his book *It Was All a Lie: How the Republican Party Became Donald Trump*, former Republican operative Stuart Stevens bemoans the current state of affairs in the party. Of his time working to elect Republicans at every level from local to national, Stevens remarks, "I was paid to win races for Republicans, and while I didn't win every race, I had the best win-loss record in the business. So yes, blame me. Blame me when you look around and see a dysfunctional political system and a Republican party that has gone insane."

Stevens can only shake his head at the direction current Republican leaders have taken:

> Watching the Republican Party is like watching a friend drink himself to death. There's a mix of sadness and anger tinged by a bit of sympathy for the misery he tries to hide. But alcoholism is a disease and political cowardice is just what it looks like: weakness and opportunism mixed with fear and self-loathing.

Stevens' is but one Republican perspective on the current state of the party. Many would disagree, most notably Trump himself, who said in April 2021:

> The key to triumphant future will be to build on the gains our amazing movement has made over the past four years. Under our leadership, we welcomed millions upon millions of new voters into the Republican coalition. We transformed the Republican Party into a party that truly fights for all Americans.

Opposing Viewpoints: Trumpism and the Future of the Republican Party presents a wide range of viewpoints that define and debate Trumpism and its effect on contemporary politics. In chapters titled "What Is Trumpism?"; "Trump's Presidency: Triumph or Failure?"; "Is Trumpism a Threat to Democracy?"; and "What Is the Future of the Republican Party?", viewpoint authors discuss Trumpism's many uses and abuses in contemporary society, and contemplate the effect that Donald J. Trump, the forty-fifth president of the United States, has had on politics, society, and international affairs. The viewpoints herein also reflect on where the Republican Party is headed in the twenty-first century, and how the party is likely to evolve.

OPPOSING
VIEWPOINTS®
SERIES

| What Is Trumpism?

Chapter Preface

In June of 2021, Chauncy DeVega, writing for the liberal website *Salon*, offered this definition of Trumpism:

> Donald Trump is no longer a mere person. Indeed, to some extent the human being behind the Trump persona has become irrelevant. For his followers—and just as much for his enemies—he represents an idea, a feeling, a worldview and a movement. We call this "Trumpism": it is a fascist and authoritarian understanding of the world, and an associated set of values and beliefs. Like other forms of fascism, it is not a coherent ideology.

DeVega's opinion may be slanted left, but his observation that Trumpism is not a coherent ideology is instructive. How else can one understand the many apparent contradictions floating about in the Trump universe? For example, Trump is opposed to almost all forms of immigration, yet two of his three wives, including former First Lady Melania Trump, were immigrants. He is opposed to chain migration, where immigrants bring their families over to the United States, but Melania Trump did just that for her parents. As Chris Frates of *CNN* writes, "It's more than a little ironic that a guy as hardline on immigration as Donald Trump has been surrounded by immigrants his entire life."

Trumpists uphold Israel's conservative government. Trump's son-in-law, Jared Kushner, is Jewish, and his daughter, Ivanka, converted to the faith. Yet anti-Semitism is rampant among his supporters, who chanted "Jews will not replace us" on one particularly memorable occasion. Trump opposes mail-in voting, yet he and many other prominent Republican elected officials typically vote that way. Trumpists are fiercely opposed to communism, yet they align with Vladimir Putin's Russian dictatorship. MAGA (Make America Great Again) enthusiasts have been seen wearing T-shirts bearing the sentiment "I'd rather be a Russian than a Democrat." The shirt is currently for sale on Amazon.com.

Many Trumpists fear that getting a COVID-19 vaccination will let the government track their whereabouts. Yet they carry their cellphones, which convey their locations at all times, around blithely. Many of the Capitol rioters of January 6 were identified by authorities precisely because they had their cell phones activated on that day.

At a time when political fandom has reached the fanatical heights associated with sports mania, those on the left and right are more divided than ever, and finding centrists is not easy. Liberals and conservatives alike have begun to resemble sports fans, who do not care whether the game is played well or fairly so long as their team wins. Trump's own fan club has reached almost absurd heights on internet sites such as Facebook, 4chan, and Reddit, as well as among some religious groups.

So here is another contradiction: Although Donald Trump may no longer be a mere person, his success owes more than any other president in modern history to a cult of personality. The cult of Trump far overshadows the kind of the fandom accorded to John Fitzgerald Kennedy or Ronald Reagan, charismatic leaders who still never attained the degree of sheer adulation showered by his fans on Donald Trump. Early in his presidency, many of Trump's online supporters began to refer to him as "God Emperor." Some say that the term is simply a tongue-in-cheek way to annoy the "libs" (liberals). But the fact that Trump attempted to stay in office despite being voted out makes the term perhaps more than a bit uncomfortable.

However much Donald Trump has energized his supporters, numbers don't lie. He has energized his opponents even more. Stacey Abrams's campaign to encourage voting in Georgia is but one example. In four years, Trump lost first the House, then the Senate, and finally his own bid for reelection. Supporters will point to his gains in the Supreme Court, which could last far longer, but when he stepped down from office in January 2020, Democrats controlled two of the three branches of government.

The Republican Party is now personified in Donald Trump. Many conservatives, such as former Secretary of State James Baker, have suggested that going forward Republicans need to focus on principles and not personality. But Trump the man is still so popular in red states and counties across the country that Republicans who desire to stay in office must embrace MAGA. They still fly to Trump's Florida estate at Mar-a-Lago to gain the imprimatur of the former president, and they are still actively attempting to dispute the 2020 election results. But Trump no longer is president and he doesn't have a Twitter account—and his influence could easily fade. When the majority of a major American party's voters and elected officials are obsequious to the whims of one man, it is only fair to wonder about the future of the Republican Party in the United States.

> *"The history of the American people is a complex saga of bloodshed for freedom from authoritarian tyranny, repudiation of an aristocracy to assure equality of opportunity, and the yearning for self-sufficiency and dignity."*

Trumpism Has Deep Cultural Roots

Geoffrey P. Hunt

In the following viewpoint Geoffrey P. Hunt argues that Donald Trump enjoyed his time in the White House because of his many successes. Hunt cites the rising stock market, which he claims has financially elevated numerous ordinary Americans. This economic revival under Trumpism has its roots in populist politics going back to the presidencies of John Tyler and James Polk. Donald Trump, though a wealthy urban businessman, identifies with the "little people," those who roll up their sleeves and get to work. He claims to understand the ordinary American. His administration takes credit for ushering in an important new era of American prosperity. Geoffrey P. Hunt is a social and cultural anthropologist who has written numerous articles for the American Thinker.

As you read, consider the following questions:

1. How does the author compare today's economic expansion with Manifest Destiny?
2. What is the author's purpose in elaborating about the painting of the jolly boatman?
3. How, according to the author, did Donald Trump improve life for everyday Americans?

President Donald Trump's occasional unfiltered coarse cloudbursts belie a man who is enormously joyful, having an abundance of entertaining good humor easily expressed, fairly shared. Trump is having a ball, for good reasons.

Trump's first year as president may have been the most extraordinary since the 1840s. While Trump has disrupted almost all presidential governance and communication norms, his tenure so far has produced capital market gains of some $7 trillion, spreading investment wealth to millions of regular Joes and Marys, while tax cuts have already distributed $3 billion in bonuses and wage hikes to over 2 million workers and counting.

The Trump-inspired American economic revival, accompanied by a cultural earthquake in newfound respect, self-esteem, and optimism for working-class citizens, rural and urban—ignored and maligned since the industrial heartland was eviscerated in the 1980s—matches the economic and territorial expansions under presidents John Tyler and James Polk.

Westward expansion, Manifest Destiny, abetted by industrial innovation from the telegraph to steam engines to sewing machines, ushered in the longest economic growth period in American history—1841 to 1859.

The 1840s also propelled the American Renaissance in literature and art. The fabulous Hudson River School of landscape painting, originating around 1825, spawned two major shifts in the 1840s: landscapes capturing Easterners' imagination about the West and illustrations of people in everyday scenes with the Americana backdrops. Perhaps the best practitioner of the new genre was George Caleb Bingham, portrait painter and politician, who lived most of his life in Missouri.

Bingham captured the heart of the American spirit—a mix of personal liberty and economic fortunes—in his iconic 1846 painting, *The Jolly Flatboatmen*, now owned by and usually on display at the National Gallery of Art.

NGA director Rusty Powell says *The Jolly Flatboatmen* is " the most important genre painting in American history."

No one knows whether Bingham's boatmen, dancing and luxuriating on the deck of a river flatboat barge loaded with furs, bolts of cloth, and other premium cargo, are floating downstream on the upper Missouri or Mississippi. The exact topography doesn't matter; the image conveying understated exuberance is infectious.

The solitary fiddler, the frying pan-tambourine man, and the other boatmen could have been figures drawn by Caravaggio, inviting the viewer to join in the moment, to take a seat on the hand-hewn oar or on top of the chicken coop—no more, no less.

Bingham's clarity of purpose matches his clarity of brushstrokes. The viewer's angle could be from a small river skiff, such as a Mackinaw boat. The closest boatman bemused at our attention seems contented enough, despite his toes sticking out from the welt of his shoe. The slightly impish man in the Quaker wide-awake hat, alongside the steering-oarsman, looks self-satisfied, confident, and prosperous enough.

Franklin Kelly, curator at the NGA, said this about "The Jolly Flatboatmen":

> It's very democratic. These are working people; they're wearing their ordinary clothes—tattered—but they're having a good time. It's that notion of a democratic art in a democratic society.

Donald Trump, the NYC luxury high rise-builder, should be the most unlikely populist egalitarian. Yet Trump would be at home with the jolly flatboatmen. These are the people who built the nation, unmolested by a suffocating federal government. By

1846, only Missouri and Iowa among the Missouri River territories had been admitted to the Union.

People of the frontier, anyplace west of the Appalachians, in the 1840s were tamers of the wilderness. Life could be nasty, brutish, and short, as wrote Hobbes in another century. Yet endurance, calculated risk-taking, commercial cleverness, and even desperation produced American pragmatism, and exeptionalism.

These are Hillary Clinton's deplorables. These are the Walmart shoppers. These are the truck-drivers, machine tool-operators, steamfitters, and grocery aisle shelf-stockers. These are the diverse line-up of Trump voters in Youngstown, Ohio, who stunned CNN about a week ago with their full-throated approval of Trump's first year.

Bingham, the painter, was no stranger to the imperfect, messy features of frontier and small-town democracy. He dabbled in politics as a Missouri state senator and Missouri treasurer, among other statewide offices.

In his *The County Election* (St. Louis Museum of Art), Bingham displays both porcelain and pockmarks on the faces of a remarkable collection of backgrounds and temperaments, where each vote is equal, the outcome accepted.

There are four sweeping themes occupying American socio-economic history: westward expansion, slavery, immigration, and industrialization. These themes have a common narrative: labor and natural resources. The narrative about labor invokes contradictory notions about liberty and submission. Moreover, the history of the American people is a complex saga of bloodshed for freedom from authoritarian tyranny, repudiation of an aristocracy to assure equality of opportunity, and the yearning for self-sufficiency and dignity.

The delivery of socio-economic justice, ameliorating the worst excesses within the labor narrative, has always been through the gifts of fertile land, "the fruited plain," an abundance of natural resources. The "peoples' history," expropriated by deconstructive historians using disingenuous storylines of labor oppression and subjugation, is really about rivers, harbors, timber, cotton, corn, wheat, coal, oil, and iron ore. Ships, sails, barges, mills, machines, furnaces, coke and coal, iron, steel, rails and roads, steam engines, trucks, tractors, and airplanes—this is the stuff of nation-building, prosperity, and empire—and ultimate redemption.

Donald Trump gets it. There are no Democrats remaining who get it. No one should underestimate Trump's legion of Jolly Flatboatmen who freely voted for their self-interest and can now dance to their own tune, all because of Donald Trump.

> *"Most would-be Trump successors will try to imitate his unique line of showmanship, braggadocio, and insult comedy, and inevitably will fall short."*

Trumpism Could Be Here to Stay

Geoffrey Kabaservice

In the following viewpoint, Geoffrey Kabaservice discusses the prospect for a restoration of Trumpism in 2024. While he observes that Trump had very few legislative wins, Kabaservice notes that for wealthy Americans, the Trump era delivered on its promises. But for the average American who could have benefited from an infrastructure push, health care reform, a reduction in income inequality, and numerous other programs, Trumpism proved a failure. Instead, Trump concentrated on culture wars, demeaning and debasing all of those who didn't agree with him. At the same time, the man who promised to drain the swamp was overseeing unprecedented corruption in government. Despite his failures, Trumpism could live on if Democrats do not deliver on their own promises of 2020. Geoffrey Kabaservice is the director of political studies at the Niskanen Center in Washington, DC, as well as the author of Rule and Ruin: The Downfall of Moderation and the Destruction of the Republican Party.

"Donald Trump Has Been Defeated. But Trumpism Could Be Here to Stay," by Geoffrey Kabaservice, Guardian News and Media Limited, November 8, 2020. Reprinted by permission.

As you read, consider the following questions:

1. Why, according to the author, did Trump win the White House?
2. What was Trump's chief legislative accomplishment?
3. How might the banner of Trumpism fly over the White House again, according to the viewpoint?

*F*inita la commedia. Donald Trump soon will be gone from the White House, if not from the news or our collective unconscious. But will Trumpism outlast Trump? And if so, what will be the impact of post-2020 Trumpism on the conservative movement and the Republican party?

Even though Trump often struggled to articulate his philosophy, if it can even be called that, his original campaign in 2016 proceeded from a number of key insights. The most important was that ever since the neoliberal era began in the 1980s, America had become two nations, divided by geography and class. The rift, as in most developed countries, grew between knowledge workers in the prosperous and socially progressive metropolitan areas that formed the hubs of the new global economy, and the conservative, non-college-educated inhabitants of rural areas and post-industrial towns.

While the "blue" areas recovered rapidly after the 2007-08 financial crisis, the situation for the left-behind "red" states and regions went from bleak to dire. The joblessness, hopelessness, family dissolution and "deaths of despair" that afflicted those areas were largely overlooked by the media and the Obama administration.

Trump, alone of the 2016 Republican presidential candidates, noticed that the party had come to represent the votes but not the interests of the white working—class. He defeated his competitors because he paid more attention to the problems of the base, offered unsubstantiated but emotionally convincing explanations for their plight, played upon their cultural and racial resentments, and rejected the worn-out Reaganite solutions touted by the rest of the field. He then went on to defeat the historically unpopular Democratic nominee, Hillary Clinton, by the slimmest of electoral college margins while losing the popular election by nearly 3 million votes.

When Trump entered the White House in January 2017, it was plausible that he might put policy flesh on the bones of the nationalist-populist synthesis he had outlined in his campaign. After all, in his first week in office, he invited the leaders of the major construction and building trades unions to the White House to discuss spending hundreds of billions of dollars on rebuilding the national infrastructure, which he correctly observed in his inaugural address had "fallen into disrepair and decay."

Trump might have rallied the Republican-controlled Congress to pass an infrastructure program along with the paid family leave and affordable childcare programs championed by his daughter Ivanka. He might have called for tax reforms to reduce income inequality by making hedge-fund managers and other financial fat cats pay their fair share, as he had pledged to do early in his campaign. He might have promoted training programs and apprenticeships for the skilled trades, or implemented an industrial policy to achieve economic independence from China, or adopted any number of other Republican ideas aimed at strengthening the beleaguered working class.

Trump, of course, did none of these things. As a culture warrior, he played to his base's appetite for social division, racial antagonism and malignant conspiracy theories. But in the economic sphere, he governed largely in the interests of the Republican party's donor class. The 2017 tax cut, which was his most significant (and nearly his only) legislative accomplishment, delivered the overwhelming majority of its benefits to the most affluent. It even preserved the carried-interest tax loophole, the Wall Street giveaway that Trump had repeatedly vowed to repeal. Trump had promised more affordable and inclusive healthcare, but he went along with the Republican congressional attempt (which came within one vote of succeeding) to repeal Obamacare and replace it with nothing.

Trump's 2016 "Make America Great Again" slogan was a powerful weapon aimed at an inequitable status quo supported by both parties. But by the fall of 2020, the Trump administration's inability to contain the coronavirus pandemic or its resulting economic damage, combined with his failure over the previous four years to implement anything resembling a populist program, meant that he could hardly run on a program of Trumpism, at least as he had defined it in 2016. All he could offer was his persona, which appealed mainly to the hard core of his supporters.

In the final analysis, Trump proved to be more a continuation than an alternative to standard Republican conservatism, at least as it has been defined since the Newt Gingrich era in the 1980s and 90s. Trump promised to drain the swamp but instead turned into the swamp. He took the conservative anti-government impulse and delivered corrupt, cruel, incompetent government. He redistributed prosperity upward and left the working class worse off. His most durable legacy will be the three US supreme court justices appointed during his presidency, but the working class is unlikely to benefit from, or even approve of, significant decisions by this new conservative majority. Although the court may overturn *Roe v Wade*, for example, such a decision would alienate the 45% of Trump's 2016 voters—largely non-evangelical, blue-collar voters—who either leaned pro-choice or held mixed views on abortion.

Nonetheless, conservatism is unlikely to return any time soon to the pre-Trump status quo. And despite his failures in office, the Trumpian faithful will say, like the communist apologists of yesteryear, that Trumpism didn't work because it was never really tried.

Might they be right? Could a repurposed Trumpism, in the years beyond 2024, succeed where Trump himself failed?

Most would-be Trump successors will try to imitate his unique line of showmanship, braggadocio, and insult comedy, and inevitably will fall short. But Trump wasn't wrong to perceive China as a competitor and threat, even if his trade and tariff responses proved largely ineffective. Trump's promise to deliver an alternative to Obamacare went unfulfilled, but he did break with conservative orthodoxy by refraining from cuts to the social security, Medicare and Medicaid programs on which the working class heavily depends. Trump's anti-establishment shtick proved hollow, but he tapped into legitimate outrage against the ways in which both parties permitted elites and special interests to capture so much of the economy through tax dodges, anti-competitive arrangements and outright corruption. The Trumpian indictment of the status quo, in other words, corresponds to reality and can't be dismissed as mere demagogy.

A 2024 Republican candidate running on circa-2016 Trumpism undoubtedly will play upon working-class fears that their wages will be undercut by unskilled immigrants. But such a candidate may at the same time repudiate Trump's racism, in recognition that the working class is multiracial and that the Republican party must reach beyond white Americans without college degrees, a group that shrank from 71% of the electorate in 1976 to 39% in 2018.

The prospects for populist-nationalist conservatism will depend, more than anything else, on Democratic performance over the next four years. If Democrats fail to address the economic plight of the working class or check the excesses of their cultural left wing, or if they allow unauthorized immigration or crime to return to past peaks, the banner of Trumpism may once again fly over the White House.

> "Now Dad has a ring shaped like
> Trump's face. His friend gave it to
> him as a joke; he wears it to annoy
> the libs. Mom's favorite prophets said
> Trump would win if they prayed
> hard enough."

Trump Inspires Religious Zeal in His Followers

Deena Winter

In the following viewpoint, Deena Winter, who grew up in a religious home, writes about how down-on-their-luck people of strong faith would support and donate to religious leaders, such as Jim Bakker, who turned out to be frauds, or who lived in mansions and drove luxury vehicles. These people would never lose their faith, even when confronted with facts that might have soured them on these religious leaders. Winter suggests that Donald Trump has followed in the footsteps of such leaders, soliciting donations to his cause and living in luxury while the facts suggest he is as fraudulent as the Bakkers. But nothing, Winter writes, could turn her true believing parents away from religion—or from their faith in Donald Trump. Deena Winter is a freelance journalist and writer who covered politics and news in Minnesota. Her work has appeared in the New York Times *and the* Wall Street Journal.

"Praise the Lord and Pass the Pipe Bomb," by Deena Winter, Minnesota Reformer, January 13, 2021. Reprinted by permission.

As you read, consider the following questions:

1. Why does Winter include details about her father's failure to support the family?
2. Why does Winter include the section on the ill health and eventual death of her siblings?
3. Why did Winter's formerly Democratic parents turn toward Republicans and Donald Trump?

Jim and Tammy Faye Bakker singing "Praise the Lord" on the TV was the soundtrack of my childhood.

As I'd get ready for school or play, Tammy Faye and her big fake eyelashes, painted-on eyebrows and glowing tan cheeks would grin and sit next to Jim, who looked like he belonged in the principal's office. They'd talk about Jesus.

I soaked it up, along with my four sisters and two brothers just trying to get through life in a town of a couple thousand in the southwest corner of North Dakota. Mom sent the Bakkers plenty of donations, I'm sure, as she did all preachers and prophets who met her approval and helped her raise seven kids while her husband went broke selling real estate in the middle of nowhere.

I didn't know it then, but there was an oil boom out there in the '70s that went bust, and took the briefly booming real estate market in Bowman, N.D., with it. Mom planted a garden about half the size of a football field, canned everything she could, and never said a word to us about Dad not being able to pay the mortgage.

She just Praised the Lord and kept it moving.

I don't remember Mom mentioning it when I was a senior in high school and Jim and Tammy Faye's televangelism empire came crumbling down amid a sex scandal and criminal indictments and news of Rolls Royces, a jet and air-conditioned doghouse.

Didn't matter. Mom continued to migrate away from the Catholicism of her youth to evangelism. And where she went, the family followed. Church became less monotonous, that's for sure. Less rote from Rome, more speaking in tongues and raised hands and closed eyes.

I did my best to go along, reading the whole Bible in junior high and losing a boyfriend who got freaked out when he would call and ask what I was doing, and I'd say "reading my Bible." I mean, nobody wanted to date a Jesus freak.

When the Bakkers crashed, they turned to fellow televangelist Jerry Falwell Sr. to take the reins. Falwell founded the Moral Majority, a powerful Christian lobby in the 1980s. My parents were receptive to the message, and converted from the Democratic–Nonpartisan League Party they'd joined while teachers to the Republican Party, primarily due to their opposition to abortion. By now, they were picketing outside abortion clinics and even our local hospital, which they believed was also performing abortions.

My parents joined a non-denominational Christian church, where evangelist Lowell Lundstrom once stopped on a swing through Bismarck. By then I was a young journalist, and asked my boss if I could cover one night of Lundstrom's revival at the Bismarck Civic Center. I wrote about his fire-and-brimstone message, then went backstage to talk to Lundstrom. He clutched my hand and listened intently, it seemed, before suddenly turning away to resume eating his cookies. I wrote about that, too.

I was a believer, but also a believer in telling the truth. That hasn't changed.

Three of my siblings had a rare form of muscular dystrophy that caused their muscles to literally waste away, putting them in wheelchairs and robbing them of vision, speech and the ability to feed themselves.

One televangelist who helped my brother Dusty and sister D'Ette get through the days was Joyce Meyer, a cocksure, straight-talking power-of-positive thinking preacher. When my brother could no longer make out our faces and his few friends dwindled and hope of marrying died, he would sit in his room and listen to Meyer's CDs, and cry out to God for help. He loved Christian rapper

TRUMPISM AS POLITICAL PHILOSOPHY

Trumpism is not the same as Trump. America contains multiple traditions typically named after some of its famous presidents including Madison, Jefferson, Wilson and Jackson. Rarely does the good of any one tradition appear without a dose of the bad of another. And vice-versa.

Focusing excessively on the flaws of President Trump—his ignorance, vulgarity, crudeness and authoritarianism—and on his political genius—to divide, fabricate, destabilize and corrupt—implies that voting him out of office will return America to its normal and better self. Not so. Trumpism is part of America. To quote Walt Whitman's poem Song of Myself: "Do I contradict myself? Very well then I contradict myself, (I am large, I contain multitudes)."

Trumpism is not an abnormality but a contemporary offshoot of America's Jacksonian tradition. Trump is easily stirred. Trumpism is not. It does not want to fight. Once it is aroused, however, it will fight ferociously. A product of the American heartland, it is anti-elitist, anti-urban and racist. Revived by Newt Gingrich and his 1994 Contract with America, in the last two decades American populism has grown on both sides of the political spectrum. After 2012, the grassroots Tea Party created an insurgency inside the Republican camp that, with Trump at its helm, eventually took over the party. A spent political force, Reaganism, far from opposing this development, has benefitted from the mobilization of millions who had been excluded from the political process. A populist surge mobilizing the Left of the Democratic party after 2016 yielded a landslide victory in the 2018 Congressional elections. Now a populist clash is looming for the 2020 Presidential election.

Trumpism has pushed aside both mainstream conservatives and intellectual neoconservatives. Thus it has changed the American conservative movement. Some parts of the Reaganist script endure: tax cuts, small government, strong military, ready acceptance of growing inequality, inaction on or outright opposition to environmental issues, and bulging deficits. New items have been added: misogyny, racial prejudice, and xenophobia.

"Does Trumpism Work as a Political Philosophy?" by Peter J. Katzenstein, WZB Berlin Social Science Center, March 20, 2019.

Toby Mac, and his mantra to "speak life," frequently dropping it on our foul-mouthed mother.

They didn't lose faith when the St. Louis Post-Dispatch published a bombshell four-part series in 2003 detailing Meyer's lavish lifestyle, including a $10 million corporate jet, $4 million estate and $20 million headquarters.

My sister D'Ette—who lives on Social Security disability income alone in a manufactured home—donated to Meyer. She doesn't regret it.

Praise the Lord.

My brother David died in 2009, and Dusty in 2015. I was there when they died in their bedrooms in a duplex that they rented from the county so Dad could be their care provider for years.

When Dusty died, Mom threw herself on his lifeless body and sobbed—both she and Dusty believed to his dying breath that he would be healed by God. He wasn't. She didn't lose faith, despite her pain.

I don't remember talking politics much in our house until FOX News arrived and Dad got hooked. He was the only one who would regularly parrot FOX talking points—until Donald Trump came along.

That's when many of my right-leaning, mostly Catholic and Christian friends and relatives in the Midwest got more engaged in politics. Since 2016, they've steadily become more brashly political in their social media posts and conversation.

FOX News sparked their interest, but Trump poured gasoline on it. He'd staked out space on the right, opposed to abortion and promising to put God back in the classroom. He had the same conservative stances as other Republicans, but they seem to love his in-your-face style. His refusal to back down. He is one of them (even though he was a Manhattan developer who probably never worked the farm a day in his life).

Now Dad has a ring shaped like Trump's face. His friend gave it to him as a joke; he wears it to annoy the libs. Mom's favorite prophets said Trump would win if they prayed hard enough (I'm paraphrasing). Roe vs. Wade will be overturned, they predicted.

A few weeks ago, Mom went to Arizona to visit her acolyte granddaughter, and they went to a Trump rally. Mom wore a red MAGA hat and shirt as they sang and protested what they saw as fraudulent election results.

They're Pentacostal Christians who believe in so-called prophets who predicted Trump would win again. Some of the prophets are beginning to regret their missed calls, including Jeremiah Johnson, who says he's now getting death threats from Christians.

Trump's televangelist pastor, Paula White famously called on angels from Africa and South America to help Trump win, and promised he would.

Former US Rep. Michele Bachmann posted a video Nov. 9 asking God to use his "strong iron rod" to "smash the delusion" that Biden won the election.

In August, both Mom and Dad contracted coronavirus (along with seemingly much of North Dakota) and Dad ended up in the hospital for 10 days. But they recovered and now Mom still often refuses to wear a mask in stores.

Trump and their religious beliefs have become inextricably entwined. Kids in cages, his "very fine people, on both sides," winking at white supremacists, porn star payoffs—none of it dissuades. They are fervently pro-life but think this whole pandemic is blown out of proportion.

While helping report a story for the New York Times this summer, I was asked to interview Trumpers who'd attended the president's Duluth rally—where it turned out he probably had COVID-19. The editor figured some of Trump's supporters would sour on him. I laughed inside, knowing that was unlikely.

My people's allegiance to Trump has created some tension, given I get paid to write the news and find the facts and separate wheat from chaff. There's a whole universe of alternative news out there now, so you can find a source to affirm whatever you believe.

They argue over what's truth and what's fiction. They don't believe me anymore. They think I'm fake news. They haven't yet called me an enemy of the people.

Few of them are on Twitter, but the conservative-dominated Facebook is popular with them, despite my repeated reminders that memes and random YouTube videos aren't news. My Twitter and Facebook feeds are two different worlds.

Now that it's become pretty clear that Trump is leaving—despite what some prophets said—they're still keeping the faith. "It's not over," my mom texted Thursday, one day after Trump supporters stormed the US Capitol. "It has only begun! Button up your overcoat!"

I interviewed a Prior Lake woman the same day, and she said similar things.

"It's not over," she said.

And so when I saw those "patriots" break through barricades in D.C. and storm the Capitol, I got it. They were like my parents, who would never storm the Capitol but haven't lost faith, even though they've been snookered by spiritual leaders their whole lives. Trump is just the latest to say one thing and do another and not lose their adulation.

It's not over. Praise the Lord.

> *"I think Republicans will look back on the deal that they made to get Trump and they will rue the day. I think he is doing generational damage not just to the country, but to the Republican Party and to the conservative cause."*

Trump Has Upended Conservatism

Eric Black

In the following viewpoint, Eric Black discusses his Zoom call with conservative Republican Peter Wehner, a so-called never Trumper who believes that Donald Trump's policies and actions are antithetical to true conservatism. Wehner is appalled not only by Trump's initiatives, but by his personal conduct and demeanor. While he does not agree with much of what Democratic candidate (now president) Joe Biden has to offer, he decided to vote for Biden because he believed the Democrat would do less damage to the country than Trump. Eric Black writes "Eric Black Ink" for MinnPost. He is the recipient of the Sigma Delta Chi Award for online column writing from the Society of Professional Journalists.

"Trump Has 'Upended Conservatism,' Says Lifelong Republican Peter Wehner at U of M Forum," by Eric Black. Originally published in MinnPost, July 30, 2020. Reprinted by permission.

As you read, consider the following questions:

1. According to Peter Wehner, how are Trump's policies anti-conservative?
2. Which of Joe Biden's beliefs does Wehner disagree with?
3. Did Joe Biden's victory result in the right's denunciation of Trump that Wehner was hoping for? Why or why not?

Lifelong Republican and honest-to-goodness conservative Peter Wehner wants his party back, and he's prepared to support Joe Biden for president this year in hopes of bringing that about. He spoke (virtually) yesterday at a University of Minnesota forum.

Wehner has been a consistent and early never Trumper.

Four years ago, before Donald Trump had secured the Republican presidential nomination but after it had become likely he would do so, Wehner—who had worked in the White House under all three of the recent Republican presidents (Reagan and both Bushes)—spoke at the U of M's Humphrey School of Public Affairs and declared himself a never Trumper.

(Wehner had actually already said the same in a New York Times op-ed piece, but I covered him at the Humphrey School in a 2016 never-Trumper talk, when he boiled it down to this:

> Mr. Trump is a toxic figure in American politics. If you want to know how toxic he is, he has a 70 percent unfavorable rating right now. And that would make him the most disliked nominee in the history of polling. Neil Newhouse, a veteran Republican pollster, said that "In the modern polling era since World War II, there has not been a more unpopular potential presidential nominee than Donald Trump." Mr. Trump is toxic for a reason. He is—in my estimation—nativist, xenophobic, cruel, vindictive, emotionally unstable, narcissistic, obsessive, and yet, he is without an economic agenda or a governing philosophy. He's stunningly ignorant on issues, and he seems to be a person who's given over to profanity and demagogy.

Four years later (meaning Wednesday), speaking over Zoom to yet another Humphrey School/Center for the Study of Politics and Governance audience, Wehner isn't taking any of it back. His updated portrayal of Trump's presidency described in stark terms key differences between a proper conservative and Trump, whom he said has "upended conservatism, as I understand the term."

Yes, conservatives got two new conservative justices on the Supreme Court, which is no small deal and has led to some rulings that conservatives like, Wehner said. But Trump is more properly understood as a populist who has stitched together some conservatism with some red meat to appeal to other elements of the electorate.

Trump, Wehner said, has "upended conservatism, as I understand the term. He's a protectionist, while conservatives have been free traders." Conservatives have been fiscally cautious, Wehner said, while "deficits and debt have exploded under Trump." Conservatives "believe in a foreign policy based on morality; Trump hasn't done that."

Furthermore, the way Trump conducts himself should also offend real conservatives, Wehner said. Conservatives believe in "epistemological humility, respect for human experience, aversion to fanaticism, a belief in the complexity of human society, a belief in objective truth and a whole range of things … [whereas] a lot of what Donald Trump has done has been an assault" on conservatism and conservative philosophy. Wehner believes Trump's personal conduct "has done great damage to conservatism and to the Republican Party. … So I don't really consider him a conservative. I consider him a populist and an ethnic nationalist" resembling some of the populist/nationalist leaders elsewhere in the world.

In summary, Wehner said: "I think he's actually broken with conservatism and redefined it in a negative way."

So, in case you hadn't already figured this out, Wehner said that although he disagrees with Joe Biden across a wide range of policy positions, he will vote for Biden in hopes of saving the country and the Republican Party from four more years of Trumpism.

That worries him too, he admitted. While he views Biden as a moderate liberal, he fears Biden will be pulled to the left by the pressures within the party. Wehner's not happy about that, and his vote will be much more anti-Trump than pro-Biden. He hopes a Biden win will enable his party to repudiate the unsavory aspects of Trumpism in the aftermath and get back to representing honest, honorable conservatism.

U of M political scientist Larry Jacobs, who moderated the event, asked Wehner how he'll feel if Biden wins and then does things that conservatives won't like, such as use the next Supreme Court opening to shore up support for Roe v. Wade/legalized abortion. Wehner was ready for that and replied:

"Yes, since I intend to vote for Joe Biden I have to recognize that he will pursue some policies that I will disagree with. … There were a number of people who at the beginning of the Trump era were conservative, and they've given up their conservatism [in reaction against Trumpism]. I'm not one of them. So I'm not an enthusiast for Joe Biden and his agenda. He seems to be an admirable human being, and that's important to me. But I quite agree" that Biden will advance many policies Wehner opposes.

And that worries him, because, he said: "I think the Democratic Party has moved from liberalism to progressivism. They are different and distinct things. And I believe there is a kind of illiberalism that's increasingly powerful in the progressive movement: the 'cancel culture,' the so-called 'woke politics.'"

He enumerated some areas that worry him about what the left might do:

"Abortion. Bill Clinton used to say 'safe, legal and rare.' You can't say that as a Democrat any more. Socialism is much more embraced. The Democratic Party has moved far to the left. So, I will, as a writer, as a public voice, be critical of Biden ….

"But I believe that if you balance the good and the bad of Trump versus the good and the bad of Biden, I come out with the scale that's very much in favor of Biden. And not because his policies are better. I think that Trump's combination—really a unique combination—of ignorance and incompetence that we're seeing manifest in this year, particularly in the COVID-19 situation. And there's the almost nihilistic assault on truth, and the damage—the radiating damage to our civic culture. And the cruelty.

"So I just think that our country will be more injured with the Trump presidency than without it. The last thing I'll say on this question is this:

"I think Republicans will look back on the deal that they made to get Trump and they will rue the day. I think he is doing generational damage not just to the country, but to the Republican Party and to the conservative cause. They will have gotten four years of some policy victories, plus some policy setbacks. But the price for that, in terms of how the Republican Party is seen, the damage to the generation, the toxicity that it's introduced, I don't think it's gonna be a close call. That why I think that conservatives, not just for the cause of conservatism, but for the country, should vote against Donald Trump. Not because they think Joe Biden will pursue policies that are fantastic but because Donald Trump is a malicious force in American life."

I hope I didn't run on too long quoting Wehner. When Trump was first rising, I just assumed that a certain number of decent Republicans would rise to the rescue just based on decency. That was four years ago now. I haven't heard too many Wehners in the intervening period. So I hope he's not the only one thinking along lines of common decency and basic honesty heading into November.

I also have to confess that there was another member of the panel that I Zoom-covered yesterday, political scientist David Hopkins of Boston College. Hopkins spoke much less and didn't offer his own views, playing the neutral analyst, and I'm afraid I have given him short shrift.

> *"The problem with cults and cultism is, and has always been, absolute worship is given to objects of worship that are somewhat or highly unworthy."*

Trumpism Is a Cult

John Nassivera

In the following viewpoint, John Nassivera traces the history of cults and cultism to draw comparisons between very early forms of religious cults and present day Trumpism, which the author considers every bit as much a cult. Cults are dangerous things, Nassivera observes. The present-day adoration of Donald Trump and the notion that he was sent by god to rule over the United States like a king goes against everything that America stands for. There is a reason the founders separated church and state, Nassivera argues, not because religion is unimportant, but because it is already so central to much of American life. Opponents of Trumpism must understand his cult for what it is in order to combat it. John Nassivera is a former professor who retains affiliation with Columbia University's Society of Fellows in the Humanities.

"On Faith: Trumpism Is a Cult," by John Nassivera, Rutland Herald, July 25, 2020. Reprinted by permission.

As you read, consider the following questions:

1. What were cults like in the Greek and
    Roman civilizations?

2. What was the original meaning of the word "catholic" and
    how does it differ from the meaning of "cult"?

3. Why is it so hard to deprogram people from cults?

We all know the old saying, "Those who do not know the past are condemned to repeat it." The fact this saying is so well-known doesn't mean it's trite or false. It isn't. It's too, too true. Trumpism is a cult and not knowing the history of cults makes one, or one's society, condemned to be victimized by a cult and a cult leader.

Our English word cult comes from the Latin "cultus," which meant the care and devotion of the gods. For the Greeks and Romans, it was always the gods, plural. One of earliest cults common among the Greeks and Romans was the "hero cult," the worship of a human who was the product of a god mating with a human woman—Heracles was the son of Zeus and Alcmene, for example. A cult hero might also be a mortal who had received special favor from the gods and was, in effect, brought into their family. There were also cults dedicated to specific nature gods, each having his or her own shrine and special location. The city of Rome had hundreds of such shrines/temples, each one having its specific group of devout followers and temple keepers. The same was true across the whole empire. It was chaos.

The early Christian "catholic" church, during its first several centuries, had to figure out how to somehow accommodate this age-old habit of cults for gods and heroes. "Catholic" was originally just the Greek word for "universal" and it was used by the Roman government and Roman law; it referred to the church under the bishop of Rome as "Catholic," meaning "Universal" throughout the empire. This was seen as a way to unify the hugely varying religious beliefs and rituals of so many widely different peoples living under Roman law.

But these old cults were very, very powerful phenomena and they did, indeed, contribute to inter-group distrust and violence. The human tendency to become a member of a cult is truly ancient, one could even say primordial. The early Church of Rome (and Constantinople) came up with a solution of genius: the acceptance and encouragement of the "Cult of the Saints."

Saints were defined (and still are defined) in Catholic teaching as humans whose lives were highly exemplary and heroic, and in death, they occupy and position closer to God than humans in general. And similar to the ancient pagan gods and heroes, the saints could then (and can now) intercede and provide special assistance to those who venerate them. Saint Mary, the mother of Jesus, is certainly the best-known saint and the very first one.

You might justifiably ask, "How much of this old stuff has anything to do with Donald Trump and Trumpism in America?" And I have to answer, "A lot, a heck of a lot." As almost everyone knows, the Cult of the Saints is something that has always been flatly and violently condemned in Protestantism all the way back to Luther and Calvin. OK, they had their reasons, I get it. But this means that the difference between types of honor and devotion has also been lost—leaving one and one's society wide open for an attack of cultism on an exposed flank. In our case, it's on the right flank.

The distinction that has been lost is God alone is to be worshiped while the saints and heroes are only to be revered, given reverence. Built into this distinction is an awareness that we must take great care regarding to whom and how we give our devotion and unwavering support. The problem with cults and cultism is, and has always been, absolute worship is given to objects of worship that are somewhat or highly unworthy.

We hear over and over again from the religious right that Trump has "been chosen by God" to lead this country. The fact such a statement is almost exactly the same as affirming "the divine right of kings" doesn't bother Trump supporters. It is worth remembering the idea was, long ago, that a king is put there by God himself in the divinely ordained system to rule over men (out-of-date gender gaffes intended). Any and all cult leaders of today make use of this socio-psychological-religious construct—even leaders of purely secular and/or atheist and/or fascist, totalitarian groups.

For all of these reasons, this word "cult" now has a largely negative connotation—and for good reason. Cults are indeed very dangerous things. This past December, one of the world's foremost authorities on cults, Steven Hassan, published a book titled *The Cult of Trump* with the subtitle "A Leading Cult Expert Explains how the President uses Mind Control." It is a disturbing but important book.

The problem of cults has been around a long, long time. In a very real sense, Christianity itself was founded and spread in order to overcome the power of cults. It was no mere accident that one of the newest and most widespread cults in the time of Jesus was the Emperor Cult, whereby each Roman emperor was proclaimed a "divifilius," "son of god," on a divine mission to rule; sacrifices to his divine spirit were mandatory in temples throughout the entire empire. Many early Christians got in big trouble for refusing to do it. It was no mere coincidence that Jesus was called Son of God: He was, via instruction by example, the polar opposite in every way to the "sons of god" who were absolute rulers of the violent Roman state.

It's not easy to deprogram the minds of cult members. We've known this for a long time now. Looking back in history, we can see clearly that it took Christianity hundreds of years to deprogram the minds of the peoples of the Roman empire. We cannot allow the minds and government of Americans to revert back to a form of politics that is 2,000 years out-of-date.

Religion and politics don't mix well together. The genius of the American Constitution was, in no small degree, the recognition of this crucial fact. This is not to say religion is unimportant. Quite the opposite. It is to say that religion is so powerful, we have to find a way to keep it out of elections and separate from the state.

"Everything old is new again," as the greatest political satirist in the English language, Jonathan Swift, said in his apropos essay "Political Lying" (printed in 1710). As Hassan has shown in excruciating detail, the core supporters of Trump have become members of a cult, in the clinical psychological-religious sense of the term. The Democratic Party and the American people have to realize this is a big part of what we are up against.

The cult of Trumpism must be stopped. This is no ordinary election.

> *"In order to return to political dominance, Republicans don't need a new candidate or to adjust their policy agenda."*

Trump Was Right, Say Conservatives

Matthew Knott

In the following viewpoint, Matthew Knott reports on the Conservative Political Action Conference (CPAC) of 2021. Though Donald Trump is no longer president of the United States, his followers still adore him, insisting Trump was right about everything and that Democrats are wrong. Many of the attendees firmly believe that Trump won the 2020 presidential election. They cite dubious statistics proving that the election was rigged. They would vote for Trump in 2024 in a heartbeat. Matthew Knott is North America correspondent for the Sydney Morning Herald *and the* Age.

As you read, consider the following questions:

1. What is the general feeling about Donald Trump at CPAC?
2. What proof do his supporters offer that the 2020 election was rigged in Biden's favor?
3. What are some of the causes Trump's followers cite as being important to them?

"'Trump Was Right': Conservatives Double Down on Ex-President," by Matthew Knott, *Sydney Morning Herald*, February 28, 2021. Reprinted by permission.

Orlando, Florida: Even before you step inside the Conservative Political Action Conference, America's largest annual gathering of right-wing activists, it's clear who commands the hearts and minds of today's Republican Party base.

A cigarette-smoking man wearing a red "Bikers for Trump" hat is circling the conference venue on an oversized tricycle. His bike is emblazoned with a sign that reads: "Trump was right about everything." A woman, wrapped in an American flag, waves a giant flag that says: "F--- Biden and f--- you for voting for him."

Inside four-star Hyatt hotel that is hosting the conference, the adoration for the former president is even more intense. The must-see attraction at this year's event is a giant, glistening golden statue of Trump wearing thongs on his feet and holding a wand.

On Monday (AEDT) the conference-goers will be able to see Trump himself, when the three-day event culminates in Trump's first speech since leaving the White House.

The artist who made the statue, Tommy Zegan, explains that it is taking a jab at former president Barack Obama, who once said of Trump's promise to bring manufacturing jobs back to the United States: "What magic wand do you have?"

This year's conference is taking place just over a month since Trump left the White House and Democrats took control of the US Senate. But it is accompanied by none of the soul-searching and internecine debates you might expect following such significant defeats.

That's because many of those attending the event do not believe Trump lost the election—despite there being no persuasive evidence of widespread voter fraud.

In order to return to political dominance, so the thinking goes, Republicans don't need a new candidate or to adjust their policy agenda: they must simply find a way to stop their opponents from cheating next time.

"It was rigged," Zegan says of the November election. "There were too many anomalies."

If Trump were to run again in 2024, Zegan says, he would definitely support him.

Anna Villalobos, who is running a stall at the conference selling MAGA (Make America Great Again) hammocks, says: "The numbers don't add up. How could 80 million people vote for Biden but only 20 million follow him on Twitter? I 100 per cent believe they stole the election."

Ronald Solomon, who runs the MAGA Mall, which sells pro-Trump paraphernalia, says he is already doing a roaring trade in "Trump 2024" flags and caps.

"If Trump wants the nomination, he gets it," Solomon says.

It's the same story on the main stage, where speaker after speaker offers the same formula for returning to power: doubling down on Trumpism.

"Let me tell you this right now: Donald J. Trump ain't going anywhere," Texas senator Ted Cruz tells the crowd to loud applause. "These deplorables are here to stay."

Florida senator Rick Scott says abandoning Trump's policies on trade, immigration and China would be like reverting to antiquated technology such as flip-phones or typewriters.

"We will not win the future by trying to go back to where the Republican Party used to be," he says. "If we do, we will lose the working base that President Trump so animated. We're going to lose elections across the county and, ultimately, we're going to lose our nation."

Florida congressman Matt Gaetz says: "We proudly represent the pro-Trump America First wing of the conservative movement. We're not really a wing, we're the whole body."

Gaetz jokes that if Liz Cheney, the Wyoming congresswoman who voted to impeach Trump last month, had been at the conference she would have been booed off stage.

"What does that say?" he asks. "The leadership of our party is not found in Washington, D.C."

As would be expected at such an event, there are panel sessions on abortion, gun ownership and foreign policy.

Big tech bias against conservatives is a major focus, with several speakers advocating breaking up social media giants such as Facebook and Google. It's an interventionist position that until recently would have been well outside the conservative mainstream.

But, by far, the dominant theme at this year's conference is election integrity.

Seven panel sessions in total are dedicated to "protecting elections", with speakers proposing a series of new measures to tighten voting rules.

"Democrats, not Republicans, installed ballot drop boxes on sidewalks, where nobody oversaw them," conservative commentator Deroy Murdock says. "How many fraudulent ballots got deposited in these boxes unchecked and then got counted? Who knows."

T. W Shannon, a former state legislator from Oklahoma, appears to justify the deadly January 6 assault on Congress by saying: "The reason that people stormed the Capitol was because they felt hopeless because of a rigged election."

Donald Trump junior, himself seen as a possible future Republican presidential candidate, delights the crowd by using air quotes when referring to Joe Biden's "80 million votes" and joking that the event should be renamed TPAC: the Trump Political Action Conference.

Offering a preview of his father's upcoming address, he says: "I imagine it will not be what we call a 'low-energy' speech. And I assure you that it will solidify Donald Trump and all of your feelings about the MAGA movement as the future of the Republican Party."

Periodical and Internet Sources Bibliography

The following articles have been selected to supplement the diverse views presented in this chapter.

Mariano Aguirre, "Trumpism, an ideology for the extreme far-right globally," *openDemocracy*, December 14, 2020. https://www.opendemocracy.net/en/trumpism-ideology-extreme-far-right-globally/.

Lee Bebout, "Trump tapped into white victimhood—leaving fertile ground for white supremacists," Conversation, January 7, 2021. https://theconversation.com/trump-tapped-into-white-victimhood-leaving-fertile-ground-for-white-supremacists-150587.

Rachel D. Beeman, "What are the three characteristics of Trumpism?: A Discourse Analysis of Trump's Four Major Campaign Speeches," *Political Analysis*, vol. xix, 2018. https://core.ac.uk/download/pdf.

Philip Bump, "How important is Trump to Trumpism?" *Washington Post*. June 7, 2021. https://www.washingtonpost.com/politics/2021/06/07/how-important-is-trump-trumpism/.

John Cassidy, "Trump May Be Gone, But Trumpism Isn't," *New Yorker*, January 22, 2021, https://www.newyorker.com/news/our-columnists/trump-may-be-gone-but-trumpism-isnt.

Ashique KhudaBukhsh, Mark Kamlet and Tom Mitchell, "Don't blame Fox News for the attack on the Capitol," Conversation, January 30, 2021. https://theconversation.com/dont-blame-fox-news-for-the-attack-on-the-capitol-154047.

Andrew Mitrovica, "Fox News is the Republican Party," *Al Jazeera*, February 7, 2021. https://www.aljazeera.com/opinions/2021/2/7/fox-news-is-the-republican-party.

Ivan Natividad, "Trump lost, but his brand of politics may be here to stay," *Berkeley News*, November 17, 2020. https://news.berkeley.edu/2020/11/17/trump-lost-but-his-brand-of-politics-may-be-here-to-stay/.

Anthony Pahnke, "On the American right, Trumpism still rules," *Al Jazeera*, May 31, 2021. https://www.aljazeera.com/opinions/2021/5/31/on-the-american-right-trumpism-still-rules.

Bill Schneider, "The troubling persistence of Trumpism," *Hill*. May 27, 2021. https://thehill.com/opinion/campaign/555590-the-troubling-persistence-of-trumpism.

Derek Thompson, "The Deep Story of Trumpism," *Atlantic*, December 29, 2020. https://www.theatlantic.com/ideas/archive/2020/12/deep-story-trumpism/617498/.

Jeff Tollefson, "Tracking QAnon: how Trump turned conspiracy-theory research upside down," *Nature*, February 4, 2021. https://www.nature.com/articles/d41586-021-00257-y.

Sean Trende, "Trumpism after Trump," *Washington Examiner*, June 17, 2021. https://www.washingtonexaminer.com/politics/trumpism-after-trump.

Jill Tucker, "Experts see cult-like behavior in Trump's most extreme followers. Breaking them free may not be easy," *San Francisco Chronicle*, January 17, 2021. https://www.sfchronicle.com/bayarea/article/Will-followers-walk-away-from-the-cult-of-Trump-15876686.php.

Anthony Zurcher, "What next for Trump—and Trumpism?" BBC. January 22, 2021. https://www.bbc.com/news/world-us-canada-55773123.

OPPOSING
VIEWPOINTS®
SERIES

CHAPTER 2

Trump's Presidency: Triumph or Failure?

Chapter Preface

Ultimately, the single most important indicator of the success or failure of Donald Trump's presidency came down to a single word: coronavirus. While his diehard supporters have suggested that Trump's response to the pandemic that ravaged the United States in 2020–2021 saved millions of lives, most objective observers, including the lion's share of medical professionals, understand that Donald Trump did very little to prevent the deaths of over four hundred thousand Americans while he was president. Trump flailed around as the virus raged across America, first underplaying the severity of the disease in his public statements (while in private it was made clear by journalist Bob Woodward that he did in fact realize that COVID-19 was deadly), then leading the country down the primrose path to disaster.

Trump continually refused to trust his own medical professionals such as Anthony Fauci, instead worrying that too much talk of gloom and doom would endanger his reelection campaign—the only thing he really seemed to care about. When Trump did confront the disease head-on in a string of press conferences designed to show that he was in charge, his ludicrous suggestions about injecting disinfectant and hitting the inside of the body with a "tremendous" light to destroy the virus left medical professionals shaking their heads in despair. Fauci was seen in one such briefing covering his face with his hand, or facepalming, as the expression goes. Shockingly, some of those who listened to Trump had to be treated at hospitals after taking him literally and drinking bleach.

There is no way to know whether Trump would have been reelected had he been realistic and truthful about the virus. His fans, of course would have voted for him even if, as he once joked, he shot someone on New York City's Fifth Avenue. But the eighty-one million people who voted for his opponent were clearly not impressed. It is not easy to dethrone a sitting president. In modern history, one-term presidents have been uncommon, though Jimmy Carter and George H.W. Bush are examples. The sitting president has the bully pulpit and, like Trump, can use it to powerful effect. Trump's loss in 2020, despite his protests that he won "by a lot," is a resounding commentary on the ineffectiveness of his regime. His advocates would argue that Trump oversaw the development of the COVID-19 vaccines, which have been rolled out mainly under Joe Biden and proven highly effective. But the truth is that the Pfizer vaccine was developed in Germany by Turkish immigrants. The Moderna vaccine was created in the United States and led in part by Kizzmekia Corbett, an immunologist at the US National Institutes of Health (NIH) and a black American. It seems that some of the very groups Trump demonized during his tenure in the White House were instrumental in saving American lives.

Trump's failed leadership during the pandemic was crystalized on Friday, October 2, 2020, when he announced that he and the first lady had themselves contracted COVID. When, after receiving the best medical care in the world, the president recovered only a few days later, he told the world that COVID-19 was not to be feared. He ripped off his face mask and declared he was immune from the disease. Many of Trump's supporters have followed his lead in dismissing the severity of the disease. Even after the vaccine was proven safe and effective, millions of Trump's true believers feared rolling up their sleeves and getting the shot—even though Trump himself was quietly vaccinated just before leaving office. As a role model for public health, Trump proved to be an abject failure once again.

Again, Trump's supporters will point to his successes: a dramatic tax cut aimed mostly at corporations and the wealthy; three conservative Supreme Court Justices; numerous other judges appointed to benches around the country; and a feeling among his acolytes that America was once again great. But the election results of November 6, 2020, don't lie (even though Trump and his supporters claim otherwise). On that date, in what must be considered a referendum on his four turbulent years in the White House, America soundly rejected Donald J. Trump.

> *"America First' seemed to promise a clear defense of US primacy in a changing world order. Today, the US has all but abdicated its position as the world's most globally engaged power."*

There Were Pros and Cons to Trump's America First Policy

Klaus W. Larres

In the following viewpoint, Klaus W. Larres lays out the good and bad of President Trump's "America First" policy. He notes that it consists of three main features: limiting global politics, dealing harshly with former allies, and engaging with autocrats. Trump's policies have diverged greatly from those of his predecessors. He considered the European Union an economic competitor instead of an ally and has treated European leaders as such. Conversely, he embraced dictators such as Kim Jong-un and in doing so unwittingly encouraged North Korea's nuclear program. Stepping away from global leadership has its consequences, and Larres expresses concern about this leadership void. Klaus W. Larres is an adjunct professor of the curriculum in peace, war and defense at the University of North Carolina, Chapel Hill.

As you read, consider the following questions:

1. How did Trump change American trading policy?
2. How has he dealt with Russia?
3. What are the ultimate consequences of the United States pulling away from global involvement?

At the Republican National Convention, supporters of President Trump's reelection bid have celebrated his attempts to build a Mexico border wall, his promise to "bring our troops home" and his pledge to end US "reliance on China."

All are components of the "America First" agenda Trump ran on in 2016. Back then, he promised to "shake the rust off America's foreign policy."

Four years later, it's clearer what this looks like in practice. As a foreign policy analyst, I find Trump's "America First" vision has had three primary strands: disengaging the US from global politics, disdaining allies and befriending autocratic leaders.

1. Exiting the Global Stage

Early in Trump's administration, the US exited the Trans-Pacific Partnership, a trade alliance of mostly Asian countries, and the 2015 Paris Climate Accords. In May 2020, with the United States leading the world in COVID-19 infections, Trump cut funding for the World Health Organization, which is spearheading the global pandemic response.

Trump prefers bilateral deals, in which the US usually is the stronger partner, to multilateral agreements in which its power is offset by many other nations.

His administration's new US-Canada-Mexico trade agreement has moderate improvements over the original North American Free Trade Agreement, including stricter labor standards in Mexico. But other pledges to replace scrapped deals with better ones remain unfulfilled.

Trump has not yet come up with a "tougher" agreement to the 2015 Iran nuclear deal, nor followed up on his pledge to "negotiate a far better" international climate deal.

As a result, the US has sat on the sidelines of major world crises and international collaborations for the past three years.

New US immigration policies like the Muslim immigration ban and refusal to grant admission to most asylum seekers, both very popular with his base and abhorred by Democrats, further isolate the country from the world.

In June, the administration even stopped issuing to immigrants most work visas and new green cards, claiming they were hurting American citizens on the job market during the pandemic. That angered major American companies like Microsoft and Apple, which depend on those international skilled workers.

Protesters at the San Francisco airport hold signs reading "refugees are welcome here" and "build bridges not walls."

2. Broken Partnerships

"America First" has led to tense relations with the European Union, which Trump referred to as a trading "foe" during the 2016 election campaign. He further alienated America's European allies when he repeatedly came out in support of Brexit—the disruptive British exit from the EU—and encouraged other EU countries to follow Britain's lead.

In 2018 he told advisers on several occasions that he was considering withdrawing the US from NATO, the North Atlantic Treaty Organization founded in 1949 to militarily protect European and US interests.

These are huge divergences from the past. All Republican and Democratic presidents since World War II have expressed strong—and crucial—support for a united Europe and for NATO.

In Asia, relations with longstanding allies are likewise frayed. Trump asked South Korea and Japan to double or even quadruple their financial contributions to keep US military bases on their soil,

AMERICA FIRST

While America's shift to unilateralism most clearly reflects the priorities of Mr. Trump, who has long believed others take unfair advantage of the US, it also reflects deeper trends in the US and elsewhere. Obama administration officials were skeptical of engagement with China by the end of the Democratic president's second term, and were frustrated with WTO overreach. Mr. Trump's treatment of Chinese companies such as Huawei Technologies as security threats, meanwhile, has won bipartisan support. Many of the president's Democratic rivals share his aversion to endless wars, and see trade pacts as giveaways to corporations that sacrificed the livelihoods of working-class Americans.

Some countries believe that the shrinkage of the US military footprint abroad started under President Obama, most notably with his decision not to punish Syria for its use of chemical weapons. In an interview with the Economist, French President Emmanuel Macron said Mr. Trump sees NATO as a commercial arrangement in which Europeans buy American products in exchange for American military protection. "France didn't sign up for that," he said. Europe, Mr. Macron said, needs to "take responsibility for more of our neighborhood security policy."

American clout in diplomatic, military and economic matters has long tamped down intra-Asian rivalries and counterbalanced China's growing presence. Presidents George W. Bush and Obama promoted the 12-country Trans-Pacific Partnership as an alliance of like-minded countries linked through American-style trade and investment rules to serve as an economic bulwark against China.

But the Trump administration saw the TPP as inherently flawed because it was multilateral, not bilateral. In multilateral deals, "We give up a lot of our leverage," Robert Lighthizer, Mr. Trump's US trade representative, told Congress in 2018. "You're in an agreement with five countries, you have a problem with one of them. What do you do? You don't get out of the agreement." The US, he said, "is far better off in bilateral deals. We have the biggest market; we have more leverage…You're the United States of America, you can enforce your rights under that agreement."

"What 'America First' Means Under Trump Is Coming Into Focus" by Greg Ip, WSJ, January 19, 2020.

apparently failing to realize that these bases give the US a strategic presence in a region dominated by China and North Korea.

America's military presence in Asia helps the US gather intelligence and respond quickly to, for instance, a North Korean nuclear attack.

3. Embracing Dictators and Autocrats

Trump believes his three meetings with North Korean leader Kim Jong-un in 2018 and 2019—a landmark initiative of his administration—fixed the North Korea threat. But most analysts find North Korea was actually emboldened by American diplomatic engagement. It is now speeding up its nuclear program.

Conciliatory behavior toward Kim is part of a trend: Trump has embraced some of the world's most notorious dictators and autocrats.

In Europe, Trump is on good terms only with the proudly undemocratic leaders of Hungary and Poland. He called Egyptian leader Abdel Fattah el Sisi "my favorite dictator" and refused to punish Saudi Arabia after Crown Prince Mohammed bin Salman was implicated in the brutal murder of the Saudi Washington Post columnist Jamal Khashoggi in October 2018. Instead, the White House permitted two US companies to share sensitive nuclear power information with the Saudis.

The administration's relations with Russia, which surreptitiously aided Trump's 2016 campaign, are unusual.

On the whole, his government has pursued a tough policy toward Russia, including imposing harsher sanctions and deploying new NATO forces to the Polish border to protect Eastern Europe.

But Trump has denied Russian interfered in the US election, and he talks to Putin more frequently than he does to allies like German Chancellor Angela Merkel or British Prime Minister Boris Johnson. In June he pressed those leaders to invite Putin to a G-7 meeting in Washington. They rejected the idea; Russia was expelled from the club of elite nations after Putin's 2014 annexation of Crimea, part of Ukraine.

Soon after, news broke that Moscow promised to pay Taliban fighters to kill American soldiers in Afghanistan. Trump dismissed US intelligence on the matter as "fake news." Several former national security officials say that Trump wishes to avoid antagonizing Putin.

Russia's President Vladimir Putin offers a 2018 football World Cup ball to US President Donald Trump.

Election 2020

Trump has no such qualms with China, a clear bogeyman of his reelection campaign. Trump has been consistently critical of China, even retaliating against what he calls unfair trade practices with his own trade war.

Though tough on the US economy, this stance has some bipartisan approval in Washington and among US allies. China's refusal to stop subsidizing many state-owned enterprises, grant greater market access to foreign firms and protect intellectual property rights are issues of great global concern, as is its increasingly assertive foreign policy. Still, many US China experts believe Trump's crude rhetorical attacks are unhelpful for finding a constructive way forward.

Even the administration's most initially promising diplomatic initiatives—engaging North Korea, ending the war in Afghanistan and seeking to normalize Israel's relationships with some of its Arab neighbors—have not resolved these chronic international crises.

Back in 2016, "America First" seemed to promise a clear defense of US primacy in a changing world order. That appealed to many voters.

Today, the US has all but abdicated its position as the world's most globally engaged power. China and Russia are busily working to fill the vacuum.

> *"As long as things are going okay for most people, Americans tolerate a president's verbal gymnastics. But when people are in trouble, even the most ardent government haters ask that famous question: "Where's the government?""*

Trump's Presidency Was a Failure

Elaine Kamarck

In the following viewpoint, Elaine Kamarck argues that in the age of mass communication, presidents began to spend more time on their public image than on actual governance. She cites examples from Kennedy to Obama. But Donald Trump has taken this difference between looking good and doing good to new heights. Spin has its limits, Kamarck writes, and reality is hard to deny. When there is fundamental incompetence on matters of great importance, voters tend to punish their leaders. Trump's handling of the coronavirus is one example of his incompetent leadership. Trump's presidency has taught us a valuable lesson about what happens when we elect leaders who are not prepared to govern. Elaine C. Kamarck is a senior fellow in the governance studies program as well as the director of the center for effective public management at the Brookings Institution. Her research focuses on the presidential nomination system and American politics.

"Trump's Failed Presidency," by Elaine Kamarck, Brookings, March 16, 2020. Reprinted by permission.

As you read, consider the following questions:

1. What examples of presidential mistakes does Kamarck cite?
2. What is her opinion of Trump's handling of the coronavirus?
3. What is Kamarck's point in discussing the vast nature of the federal government?

Trump's presidency is failing rapidly. Like others before him, modern American presidents fail when they cannot master or comprehend the government that they inherit. This is a hard concept to grasp in an age when non-stop media coverage leads us to focus on the president's communication skills and when presidents themselves value spin more than expertise. But in the end presidential failure is about reality, not words—no matter how lofty and inspiring or how crude and insulting.

Contemporary presidents are especially prone to mistaking spin for reality for several reasons. First of all, they are nominated not by other elected officials who have some sense of what it takes to govern, but by activists and party electorates who value inspiration and entertainment. Second, the importance of mass communication leads presidents to believe that the words and activities that got them into office can work once they are in office: more rallies, more speeches, more tweets, and more television advertising.

Nothing can be further from the truth.

Presidential scholars have been aware of the disjuncture between campaigning and governing for some time now. More than a decade ago, Sam Kernell wrote a book called *Going Public: New Strategies of Presidential Leadership* (CQ Press, 2007), in which he showed that beginning with President Kennedy, modern presidents spent a great deal more time on minor presidential addresses and on domestic and international travel than their predecessors. All this communication, he argued, came at the expense of actual governing. Later on another presidential scholar, George C. Edwards III, writing in *Overreach: Leadership in the Obama Presidency* (Princeton University Press, 2012) argued that Obama thought he could go directly to the public to get support for his programs, an approach that placed communication over negotiation and that resulted in a stunning midterm loss for his party.

Reality still matters, and spin has its limits—even in an era of social media.

As long as things are going okay for most people, Americans tolerate a president's verbal gymnastics. But when people are in trouble, even the most ardent government haters ask that famous question: "Where's the government?" And for most Americans, the president is the government. Following the botched federal response to Hurricane Katrina in 2005, the collateral damage to the presidency of George W. Bush was extensive. His popularity never recovered and his second-term agenda, including bold changes to Social Security, was destroyed. Nearly a decade later when President Obama rolled out his signature achievement, the Affordable Care Act, the hugely embarrassing crashing of the computer systems meant to implement the act increased Republican opposition to it and undermined public confidence in the government's ability to implement important executive actions.

Trump's failures during the coronavirus pandemic run the gamut from the rhetorical to the organizational. Every time the president speaks he seems to add to the fear and chaos surrounding the situation: telling Americans it was not serious by asserting his "hunches" about data, assuring people that everyone would be tested even when there were very few tests available, telling people that we are very close to a vaccine when it is anywhere from 12 to 18 months away, mistakenly asserting that goods as well as people from Europe would be forbidden from entering the United States, and announcing that Google had a website for testing while the initiative was merely an unimplemented idea, were just a few of his televised gaffes. After every presidential statement, "clarifications" were needed. Trump has the unique distinction of giving a national address meant to calm the country that had the effect of taking the stock market down over 1,000 points.

We have come to expect verbal imprecision and outright lies from this president, but that is more easily corrected on less momentous developments. When there is fundamental incompetence on matters of tremendous importance, voters punish poor results. And this is where Trump's actions on the coronavirus have gone far off target. One of the most glaring deficiencies of his administration has been the failure to have enough tests available to identify those infected and to screen others for possible exposure. South Korea, a country a fraction of the size of the United States, is testing thousands more people a day than the United States. The failure to produce tests quickly will go down as one of the biggest failures in the overall handling of this disease because it prevented authorities from understanding the scope of the pandemic and therefore made it difficult for them to undertake appropriate steps to mitigate its spread. Other countries had tests and now state governments are rapidly rolling out their own tests after the CDC belatedly removed regulatory barriers. Even the nation's chief infectious disease doctor, Anthony Fauci, has admitted that testing is a major failure—a statement that is most certainly not one of the president's talking points.

In this and other areas, Trump has failed to learn from the failures of his predecessors. When President Ronald Reagan signed into law the fundamental restructuring of the military known as the Goldwater-Nichols reforms,[1] he did this knowing that he did not want a military fiasco on his watch like the failed Iranian rescue mission that did in Jimmy Carter's presidency. And following the total breakdown in the Federal Emergency Management Agency's handling of Hurricane Katrina, President Barack Obama made sure his FEMA director was an experienced state emergency management director. He knew that poor performance during natural disasters would doom his presidency.

During the Obama Administration, the White House dealt with a precursor of the coronavirus: the Ebola virus. While the scrambling eventually worked out thanks to decisive executive

HIGHS AND LOWS OF THE TRUMP ADMINISTRATION

In the latest Yahoo News/YouGov Poll, voters reflected on what they think are the greatest accomplishments and failures of the Trump administration.

The Trump Administration's Greatest Accomplishments

Boosting the stock market tops the list of ten issues the survey asked respondents to judge the Trump administration on, with most voters (54%) considering it a "major accomplishment." One in three (35%) Biden supporters begrudged the president this achievement—far more than did so for any other.

While Trump supporters are much more likely to consider boosting the stock market a major achievement (80%), this only places it fifth on their list.

For the largest number of the president's backers (92%), the greatest achievement of the Trump administration has been creating jobs, followed by lowering taxes (84%).

The Trump Administration's Greatest Failures

Registered voters are most likely to label managing COVID-19 (62%) and preserving the environment (60%) the greatest failures of the Trump administration.

Biden voters also consider both of these issues to represent the administration's greatest failures (at 91% and 84% respectively), although "helping Black Americans" ties for joint-second place.

For their part, Trump supporters are most likely to say the administration's greatest failure is their lack of success in "draining the swamp," at 22%.

"The Greatest Achievements and Failures of the Trump Administration, According to Voters," by Candice Jaimungal, YouGov, October 10, 2020.

office leadership, it illustrated that pandemics were a fundamental national security threat. They created the Global Health Security Team in the National Security Council to prepare. In May of 2018, Trump disbanded the team allegedly because he never thought pandemics would happen and because "I'm a business person. I don't like having thousands of people around when you don't need them." Trump's hurried justification for abandoning a unit (that was well short of thousands) showed Trump's limited understanding of why government is different from business—it is in the business of preparing for low-probability events. For instance, the United States military spends billions every year preparing for wars all over the globe and even in outer space that may never take place. The art of presidential leadership is anticipating major problems and coming up with plans to mitigate them.

In addition to learning from past administrations, presidents need the ability to anticipate reactions to their actions. The Trump administration has been especially inept on this dimension from the beginning. The first big executive order he issued, largely banning Muslims from coming to America, was so ill-conceived that chaos broke out in airports around the world as people with green cards to work in America and Muslims who had assisted US military forces in Iraq were initially turned away. Airport chaos seems to be a specialty of the Trump administration. It reappeared this past weekend, as Americans came home from Europe in huge numbers following Trump's announcement to close off travelers from Europe and screen returning Americans. When travelers arrived, they found vastly inadequate staffing at airports and were thus forced into the very situation medical authorities were warning against: large crowds being hoarded into small spaces with constant, close contact.

Trump has also failed to fill top government positions and turnover is far higher than in any other recent administration, as Katherine Tenpas has tracked on these pages. The absence of expertise in top government jobs is especially dangerous during emergencies.

Also, when positions are filled they have not necessarily gone to the strongest candidates. Take for instance leadership at the Centers for Disease Control and Prevention, the nation's top agency for infectious diseases. Dr. Robert Redfield's appointment was opposed by the Center for Science in the Public Interest which warned the administration that Redfield lacked a public health background and that he was under investigation for scientific misconduct.

Modern presidents inherit an enormous enterprise called the federal government that employs about the same number of people as the 6 largest US companies and has a combined annual revenue that is larger than the combined revenues of the top 16 companies in the Fortune 500.[2] No wonder modern presidents have had trouble managing this enterprise—in an organization this big, something is always going right and something is always going wrong. A president who understands what's going right can call on deep wells of expertise to protect himself from the failures that will inevitably be attributed to him. And on the flip side, a president who is aware of what's going wrong can take corrective actions and try to stave off the kinds of bureaucratic meltdowns that will also be attributed to him.

As Oval Office leadership fails while the pandemic spreads, governors, mayors, university presidents, religious leaders, business executives, and health providers are stepping into the leadership vacuum that has been the Trump presidency. They have sent workers home to telework, announced their own social distancing rules, and developed their steps to limit the spread of the pandemic. This tragedy teaches us many things about preparedness and public health, but it also warns us about the dangers of presidents who are manifestly unprepared to govern.

Endnotes

[1] These were named after Senator Barry Goldwater (R-Ariz.) and Congressman William Nichols (D-Ala.) and established a new era of joint activity and preparation among the branches of the United States military.

[2] Elaine C. Kamarck, Why Presidents Fail and How they Can Succeed Again, Brookings Institution Press, 2016, page 123.

> "Space is too critical for the nation's defense not to have an organization that speaks for its importance, defends it against all comers, and jealously advocates for new missions and new responsibilities."

The United States Needs a Space Force

Douglas Loverro

In the following viewpoint, Douglas Loverro defends President Donald Trump's creation of a Space Force. Space, he writes, has been militarized for a long time, and Trump's recognition of this notion is an important step in dealing with other countries as they vie for superiority in outer space. Laverro provides a brief history of the militarization of space and cites reasons why the US Air Force is not equipped to deal with outer space. He concludes by stating that space is too vital to US interests to not have its own dedicated military branch. Douglas Loverro has served as NASA's associate administrator for the Human Exploration and Operations Mission Directorate and worked for the US Department of Defense and the National Reconnaissance Office.

"Why the United States Needs a Space Force," by Douglas Loverro, Space News, June 25, 2018. Reprinted by permission.

As you read, consider the following questions:

1. What were some of the initial reactions to Trump's creation of a Space Force?
2. In what ways was space militarized long before Trump's Space Force?
3. Why is the Air Force ill-equipped to deal with space issues?

S pace needs jealous advocacy. When the Chinese shot down their own satellite in 2007, Air Force and other DoD leaders were heard saying that there was no way to defend space.

The president got it right. We need a Space Force. Space is too critical for the nation's defense not to have an organization that speaks for its importance, defends it against all comers, and jealously advocates for new missions and new responsibilities. Space is too crucial to national security to be stalled by a lack of focus and an unwillingness to respond until pushed.

President Trump on June 18 ordered the Pentagon to create a separate military service to focus on national security space. Outside a cohort of people who have worked this issue for many years, the announcement was met with a different mixture of reactions—Star Wars humor, political derision and interservice sarcasm. The reactions reveal a broad misunderstanding of what a Space Force would do or what it would look like.

The most common critique was that the president had suddenly militarized space. He hadn't. That process began decades ago under President Eisenhower.

In the National Aeronautics and Space Act of 1958, President Eisenhower and the Congress created NASA to control all US space activities except those "peculiar to or primarily associated with the development of weapons, military space operations, or the defense of the United States." That military job was handed to the Department of Defense. That same year, DoD created the Advanced Research Projects Agency (ARPA then, Defense ARPA or DARPA now) specifically to prevent the kind of technological surprise that Sputnik represented. ARPA quickly became the lead for all military space activities. While work actually took place in the Army, Navy, and Air Force, ARPA guided it; and over the next decade, just about every military mission we do today in space was birthed and tested.

While in a classic sense many of those missions did not appear to be military weapons, they quickly became an integral part of the way the US planned to execute war, specifically nuclear war. And in the nation's first space policy, National Security Council Planning Board memo 5814, Eisenhower envisioned that "The effective use of outer space ... will enhance [our] military capabilities.

Military uses of outer space would include anti-ballistic missiles; communications, weather and navigation; defensive outer space vehicles; and even bombardment from space. Space has been militarized from the very beginning. And that's a good thing. Over the decades, those military space missions have saved tens of thousands of American, allied, and non-combatant lives, led to dramatic decreases in collateral damage, and allowed the US and others to provide swift and timely responses to humanitarian needs and security crises worldwide.

Many of the president's detractors pointed out, incorrectly, that the Outer Space Treaty reserves space for only peaceful purposes, but that's just not true. It is true that the treaty specifically restricts the Moon or other celestial bodies for peaceful purposes, but it was intentionally silent with regards to outer space — simply because the two major signatories, the United States and the Soviet Union, were already using space for military applications and planned to continue to do so into the future.

But these points don't really answer the questions on the minds of most Americans, "Why do we need a Space Force? Doesn't the Air Force already do this job? Isn't this just more, new unnecessary bureaucracy?"

In a word, no.

What the president proclaimed was not the beginning of the militarization of space, nor the start of a space arms race, but rather that military professionals who concentrate on space needed their own organization to truly focus their efforts on a singular task—to protect and defend US and allied interests in space and to assure their other service brethren never find themselves lacking the space support they need. To do that would require a career of training, experiences, motivations, and insights, and a mixture of skills and specialties with a focus on space, that can't be developed within the constraints of the current military branches. To develop the proper culture of space professionals who marry their personal and organizational identity to this domain, and jealously advocate for its advancement, takes more than a loose assemblage of individuals from different career fields who dabble in space during their career, but all too often view space as an assignment rather than as a home.

Lessons from Army Air Corps

This idea, that military space requires an organization of its own to reach its true potential for the nation is not a new concept. It's the exact same argument made in the 1930s by Army Air Corps leaders as to why the nation required a separate Air Force, one not focused on the business of the Army, but rather, the air defense of the nation. As one of those founding leaders General Frank Andrews, a revered Air Force pioneer for whom Andrews Air Force base is named, wrote:

"I don't believe any balanced plan to provide the nation with an adequate, effective Air Force… can be obtained…within the War Department [Army]…and without providing an organization, individual to the needs of such an Air Force. Legislation to establish such an organization…will continue to appear until this turbulent and vital problem is satisfactorily solved."

Andrews knew what any organizational theorist knows, that these twin ideas of "organizational identity" and "jealous advocacy" are the crucial elements in the success of any enterprise.

Organizational identity pushes organizations to defend and define the rationale for their own existence, anytime that existence is threatened or questioned. In the 1860s, when the first US naval vessel was sunk by a new machine called a submarine, the Navy did not retreat from the water; rather it developed a whole new school of undersea warfare. Similarly, when naval relevance was called into question at the end of the Cold War, the Navy discovered that there was an entirely new mission for it to execute—littoral operations.

Jealous advocacy works in a similar fashion to shape and strengthen an institution. Institutions that understand their domain and can see future changes and potential threats, jealously advocate for changes to their mission to stay in the lead. They do so in a bureaucratic struggle for resources and importance. As the role of unmanned aerial vehicles began to grow during operations in Afghanistan and Iraq, and services other than the Air Force began to fly them, Air Force leadership made the argument that only they should fly UAVs.

At the end of the day, they lost that fight and other services retained their own UAVs. But the point is the Air Force saw UAV operations as its mission and jealously advocated that position. Just as generations before, early air leaders had jealously advocated for an air service, which became the Air Force. It's a dynamic at play in every bureaucratic structure and that competition keeps every piece strong.

But these fundamental forces have thus far been absent from space. When the Chinese shot down their own satellite in 2007, both Air Force and non-Air Force leaders throughout the Pentagon could be heard saying that there was no way to defend space, and that we should move to non-space alternatives. The Air Force, in fact, famously initiated a series of exercises labeled "a day without space" so they could figure out how to conduct air operations without space capabilities. How different from the Navy's submarine experience where the threat was met not by retreat, but by boldly pioneering a new means of warfare.

Space Not Part of Air Force Identity

In fact, in the seven years after the Chinese attack, from 2007 till 2014, the Air Force had yet to even begin to articulate the need to respond, much less begin to change their structure or their budget to do so. It took action from space advocates in the office of the secretary of defense, rather than on the Air Staff, to begin that change.

The Air Force failed to identify space as essential to their identity. A Space Force would have had no such qualms. A Space Force would have used the opportunity of the threat to push even harder and faster to defend US space assets, not engage in a retreat—because if they did not, they would no longer matter.

Similarly, while the Air Force jealously advocates for more and more resources for air operations, and consistently attempts to expand its mission space to engage in new areas of warfare, it consistently tries to shed space missions as unnecessary or unessential.

Such was the case when the Air force failed to craft a future space weather program after the cancellation of their joint effort with NOAA in 2010, famously cancelling the launch of an already built and paid for half billion-dollar weather satellite, DMSP-20. And as the Air Force grudgingly moved to respond to the threats in space they were forced by DoD to address, they adopted a strategy that viewed that move as a zero-sum game. Future reduced capabilities would be provided to the other services in exchange for space defense, coining the term, "warfighter essential requirements" as shorthand for the cuts. A space service would have demanded increased resources and would have promised even more valuable services rather than fewer.

The difference in action and impact is most clearly seen today in the DoD-congressional struggle that is playing out in the field of missile defense. Remarkably, the service least invested in missile defense—that has almost zero dollars or people—is the Air Force, the same force that is supposed to defend the space through which every missile flies. The Congress has been pushing DoD to structure a space-based missile defense sensing system for the last four years. In any sensical world, the service that "owned" space would be arguing strongly for that mission, those needs, and by extension, those resources. They would insist that they owned that mission in the same way that the Air Force insisted it owned UAV operations. Yet, in their actual legislative proposal, the Air Force was silent on the mission, and their internal plans reveal that they would cede that mission to the Missile Defense Agency and use it to reduce the cost of the Air Force's own future space missile warning system.

Now while it may be true that MDA is the best place for such a system, this reaction is the exact opposite of jealous advocacy and organizational identity. A true space service would fight for that mission and push it more quickly and more aggressively. And the tragedy of this is not that the Air Force gets less money, it's that the nation gets less missile defense. The internal, messy, lack of identity and advocacy mean things get done more slowly, resources fail to be moved to areas of importance, other nations catch up, and the US lead shrinks.

Space is too vital for the nation to not have a military service devoted to the idea that its singular job is to keep the US in the lead. The Air Force has done a fine job of birthing US space services, but it will take a Space Force to rocket them to the forefront.

> *"US military services all have strong warrior cultures that emphasize offensive weapons and decisive lethal operations. This is as it should be. But it is not clear that the same attitude is optimal for space operations."*

The United States Does Not Need a Space Force

Michael E. O'Hanlon

In the following viewpoint, Michael E. O'Hanlon argues that the United States does not need a Space Force. Even if a Space Force is a part of the Air Force, it would still be costly and relatively tiny compared with the other military branches. O'Hanlon writes that space is an increasingly important priority for the armed forces, but a knee-jerk reaction such as Space Force is not the answer. The best course, O'Hanlon believes, is to work within the system as it is and concentrate on relatively overlooked areas such as space. Michael O'Hanlon is a senior fellow and director of research in foreign policy at the Brookings Institution, where he specializes in US defense strategy, the use of military force, and American national security policy.

"The Space Force Is a Misguided Idea. Congress Should Turn It Down," by Michael E. O'Hanlon, Brookings, April 20, 2019. Reprinted by permission.

As you read, consider the following questions:

1. What would be the size and cost of Space Force?
2. Why does the author compare Space Force to the Department of Homeland Security?
3. Where does the author give credit to the Trump administration?

With the Trump administration and thus the Pentagon now firmly behind it, and with Americans naturally predisposed to new high-tech frontiers, the proposal to create a Space Force within the US military now has lots of momentum. But Congress, which must approve the plan before the new military service is created, should say no to this alluring, misguided idea.

Some of the arguments against a Space Force, which would be bureaucratically positioned within the Department of the Air Force, just as the Marine Corps is technically part of the Department of the Navy, are mundane and largely about economics and efficiency. Others are more conceptual and strategic. Together, they add up to a strong case for skepticism.

First, the Space Force would be not just small relative to any other service but tiny. It would consist of perhaps 15,000 to 20,000 personnel, including civilians. By contrast, the Marine Corps, far and away the smallest of military services, has about 185,000 active-duty Marines. Even the Coast Guard, within the Department of Homeland Security, has more than 40,000 active-duty personnel and a grand total of nearly 90,000 employees.

Because a stand-alone military service, even if within the Air Force, will need its own hierarchy, doctrine, schools, uniforms and everything else under the sun that goes with a stand-alone organization—including, perhaps, marching bands—we will spend lots of time in the early years simply building it, at a cost the Pentagon estimates at $2 billion over five years (which seems a lowball estimate).

The experience of building other new governmental organizations should make us wary of bureaucratically reorganizing our way to a new national priority. Yes, space is a priority for the armed forces, and yes, space is a dynamic theater where adversaries are increasingly active. But after 9/11, we similarly agreed to create a Department of Homeland Security. Nearly two decades later, the verdict is still out about the wisdom of that move.

Already, the nation's top military advisory body, the Joint Chiefs of Staff, has seven members—the chairman, vice chairman, head of each of the four Defense Department services and head of the National Guard Bureau. This group does not need an eighth member and eighth separate military advisory voice.

Proponents of the Space Force argue that such a branch would be necessary to promote space-related defense projects and technology. While the Air Force does tend to be run by fighter pilots who often emphasize jet technology, it also has an institutional proclivity to play down the importance of bomber forces, unmanned systems and other technologies. The Navy might similarly overemphasize aircraft carriers while underemphasizing unmanned systems. But we cannot create a new service for each partially neglected area of the armed forces.

The best solution is for civilians, and the chairman and vice chairman, to take more of a role in promoting officers within the existing services who have a variety of specialties, and for Congress to properly fund the full range of military priorities. We have seen this approach work in the past, even with less sexy areas of technology such as long-range transport aircraft. It can work for space, too.

The Trump administration is right to create a new space command—that is, a unified headquarters of perhaps 500 to 1,000 people from across the military services who will specialize in space operations, which have in fact become much more important over the years. But Space Command will likely work best if its personnel also have strong ties to the military services, since each service ultimately depends upon the sensors, communications systems and networks operating in and through space. Integration should be the watchword.

Space systems are increasingly vulnerable today, and while we can mitigate this trend by dispersing more capabilities across large numbers of smaller satellites, space will never again be a military sanctuary. As such, most space systems today need backups of one type or another that would operate in the air or another medium closer to Earth. Again, integration of space capabilities with other assets should be the watchword. Creating a new bureaucracy might run counter to this by increasing stovepiping rather than teamwork.

US military services all have strong warrior cultures that emphasize offensive weapons and decisive lethal operations. This is as it should be. But it is not clear that the same attitude is optimal for space operations. While we should assume that adversaries will target our satellites in war—and while we need ways to counter theirs, too—we should attempt restraint wherever possible in weaponizing space, which is still humanity's last great frontier and serves the US military best as a region for creating and transmitting data rather than fighting. Creating a Space Force might run counter to this goal.

Yes, there is lots of military work to do in space, and yes, we need to devote more military attention and resources to this region. But a Space Force is not the best solution to this problem.

"There are people that don't have jobs because of tariffs but they don't know it."

Trump's Trade War Failed to Restore Manufacturing Jobs

Brad Polumbo

In the following viewpoint Brad Polumbo argues that Trump's trade war—one of his campaign promises—failed to boost the economy. Trump's intent was to reverse a decline in US manufacturing, but the tariffs he imposed failed to boost employment in the manufacturing sector. The author explains that, according to economists, tariffs do not work and in fact kill more jobs than they create. Trump could have predicted this outcome if he had paid attention to economists. Brad Polumbo is a libertarian-conservative journalist and policy correspondent at the Foundation for Econmic Education.

As you read, consider the following questions:

1. Why did Trump impose tariffs on Chinese goods?
2. What are tariffs?
3. Why were economists unsurprised by the effects of the Trump tariffs?

President Trump was elected on an anti-trade agenda in 2016, and promised that tariffs and protectionist measures could restore the US manufacturing sector. After winning the White House, the president imposed tariffs on hundreds of billions of dollars worth of Chinese goods meant to discourage imports in pursuit of this goal. He has described himself as a "tariff man" and said that "trade wars are good and easy to win."

How is this rhetoric holding up?

Well, a new Wall Street Journal data analysis sheds light on the trade war's results so far. They aren't pretty.

"President Trump's trade war against China didn't achieve the central objective of reversing a US decline in manufacturing, economic data show," reads the report.

"Another goal—reshoring of US factory production—hasn't happened either," the Journal continues. "Job growth in manufacturing started to slow in July 2018, and manufacturing production peaked in December 2018."

Trump's tariffs did not successfully promote employment in the manufacturing sector. Much of the manufacturing job gains that did occur during the president's tenure happened before the tariffs even took effect.

This news is dismaying, but it's hardly surprising.

Economists overwhelmingly agree that tariffs, which are basically taxes on American consumers, don't work. In a 2016 survey of economists, zero agreed that adding tariffs on certain goods would successfully encourage domestic production. A whopping 93 percent disagreed or strongly disagreed, while 7 percent did not answer.

"Tariffs that save jobs in the steel industry mean higher steel prices, which in turn means fewer sales of American steel products around the world and losses of far more jobs than are saved," famed free-market economist Thomas Sowell explained in one example of how tariffs backfire.

"The benefits of a tariff are visible," Nobel laureate Milton Friedman similarly noted. "Union workers can see they are 'protected.' The harm which a tariff does is invisible. It's spread widely. There are people that don't have jobs because of tariffs but they don't know it."

This is why populist-sounding politicians can boast about "protecting American jobs" and seem to the untrained eye to be telling the truth.

Yet as economists agree, the problem with tariffs generally speaking is that they kill more jobs than they create. For every job that is "protected" by a tariff, other jobs are lost in related industries that use the targeted good as an input and see their costs raised. But even within the manufacturing sector, these tariffs failed.

Why? It's simple: The tariffs helped some manufacturers by hurting others via raised prices, and (predictably) triggered retaliatory tariffs from China that together outweighed any benefits.

"An industry-by-industry analysis by the Federal Reserve showed that tariffs did help boost employment by 0.3%, in industries exposed to trade with China, by giving protection to some domestic industries to cheaper Chinese imports," the Journal reports.

"But these gains were more than offset by higher costs of importing Chinese parts, which cut manufacturing employment by 1.1%," the analysis continues. "Retaliatory tariffs imposed by China against US exports, the analysis found, reduced US factory jobs by 0.7%."

Many Americans of good faith might be earnestly surprised by how tariffs have failed to restore the manufacturing sector. But students of economics shouldn't be.

Periodical and Internet Sources Bibliography

The following articles have been selected to supplement the diverse views presented in this chapter.

Swaminathan S. Anklesaria Aiyar, "View: What will be Donald Trump's legacy? Here's a look at his major achievements and failures," *Economic Times*. November 6, 2020. https://economictimes.indiatimes.com/news/international/world-news/view-what-will-be-donald-trumps-legacy-a-look-at-his-biggest-achievements-and-failures/articleshow/79027319.cms?from=mdr.

Gerald Baker, "There's as Much to Learn From Trump's Success as His Disgrace," *Wall Street Journal*, January 17, 2021. https://www.foxnews.com/opinion/learn-trump-success-disgrace-gerard-baker.

Jacob Bor, David U. Himmelstein and Steffie Woolhandler, "Trump's Policy Failures Have Exacted a Heavy Toll on Public Health," *Scientific American*. March 5, 2021. https://www.scientificamerican.com/article/trumps-policy-failures-have-exacted-a-heavy-toll-on-public-health1/.

Steve Cortes, "Trump's Top 10 accomplishments of 2020 (Opinion)," *Lehighvalleylive.com*, Jan. 1, 2021. https://www.lehighvalleylive.com/opinion/2021/01/trumps-top-10-accomplishments-of-2020-opinion.html.

John Dunbar, "The 'Citizens United' Decision and Why it Matters," Center for Public Integrity, May 10, 2018. https://publicintegrity.org/politics/the-citizens-united-decision-and-why-it-matters.

Wendell Griffen, "Our national curse: the cruel convergence of Trump's presidency and the COVID-19 pandemic," *Baptist News Global*. April 20, 2020. https://baptistnews.com/article/our-national-curse-the-cruel-convergence-of-trumps-presidency-and-the-covid-19-pandemic/#.YQr0Gi2cZTY.

Richard Haass, "Donald Trump's Costly Legacy," Jan 11, 2021. Project Syndicate. https://www.project-syndicate.org/commentary/donald-trump-costly-legacy-three-failures-by-richard-haass-2021-01.

Victor Joecks, "Trump gave conservatives plenty to be thankful for," *Las Vegas Review-Journal*, November 26, 2020. https://www.

reviewjournal.com/opinion/opinion-columns/victor-joecks/
trump-gave-conservatives-plenty-to-be-thankful-for-2192145/.

John Haltiwanger, "Trump's biggest accomplishments and
failures from his 1-term presidency," Business Insider, Jan
20, 2021. https://www.businessinsider.com/trump-biggest-
accomplishments-and-failures-heading-into-2020-2019-12.

Elaine Kamarck, "Trump's failed presidency," *Brookings*. March
16, 2020. https://www.brookings.edu/blog/fixgov/2020/03/16/
trumps-failed-presidency/.

Robert Knight, "Giving Trump's accomplishments their due," *Washington
Times*, May 6, 2018. https://www.washingtontimes.com/news/2018/
may/6/giving-trumps-accomplishments-their-due/.

Michael Kruse, "How Trump Succeeds Without Succeeding,"
Politico, April 23, 2017. https://www.politico.com/magazine/
story/2017/04/23/why-trump-really-believes-hes-the-most-
successful-president-ever-215063/.

Politico Staff, "30 Things Donald Trump Did as President You
Might Have Missed," Politico. January 18, 2021. https://www.
politico.com/news/magazine/2021/01/18/trump-presidency-
administration-biggest-impact-policy-analysis-451479.

White House, "Trump Administration Accomplishments," White
House, January 2021. https://trumpwhitehouse.archives.gov.

Rhiannon Williams, "Donald Trump's greatest successes and failures,
from healthy markets to blatant racism," inews, November 8,
2020. https://inews.co.uk/us-election-2020/donald-trump-
greatest-success-failure-healthy-markets-racism-753418.

CHAPTER 3

Is Trumpism a Threat to Democracy?

Chapter Preface

Donald Trump's delusional notion that he won the 2020 Presidential election "by a lot" has come to be known as "The Big Lie" in Democratic and mainstream journalistic circles. The word "big" apparently distinguishes it from the many smaller lies with which Trump peppered America during his presidency. Fox News, OANN, Newsmax and other conservative platforms will never use the phrase, and Trump's many supporters, perhaps not the seventy-four million who voted for him, but a sizeable percentage of them, still fervently believe that their man was victorious.

President Trump's most ardent supporters, including QAnon and those in protest groups such as the Proud Boys, the Three Percenters, and the Oathkeepers who protested at the Capitol, were convinced that Trump would somehow be reinstated as president, if not on January 6, then surely in August of 2021. Trump himself told anyone who would listen that the reinstatement scenario would occur. But the US Constitution has no such provisions, and Trump's reinstatement date is likely to keep being pushed back, perhaps until the day he dies, by true believers.

All of the above might be laughable if it were not for the complicity of elected Republican officials who, fearing the wrath of Trump if they did not continue to push his big lie, have lined up to promote their own attacks on democracy. Using the excuse Trump provided, that the election was fraudulent, Republican legislatures in state after state have sought to pass laws making it more difficult to vote. Republicans have long known that they do far better in elections with low turnouts. This is why in non-presidential elections, when fewer voters bother to turn out, Republicans tend to see results that swing in their favor.

Given that the 2020 Presidential election hinged on the large turnout of African Americans and other minorities, including Native Americans in some states, Republicans have enacted laws specifically directed at such minorities, closing polling places in urban areas, restricting early voting days, and limiting mail-in voting. Democrats argue that everyone must be allowed to vote, and this seems reasonable in a democracy. Their argument is self-serving, in that Democrats know that larger turnouts favor their candidates. But of course, in a democracy, they are correct. Everyone should be allowed to cast a ballot in the United States of America, which touts "liberty and justice for all" and not just the favored few.

It seems a radical, almost unthinkable notion, but some Republican conservatives are turning away from democracy in an attempt to preserve minority rule. In a country with changing demographics, Republicans have two clear options by which they can maintain power: either move toward the center and attract more independents and so-called Reagan Democrats or restrict the votes directed at Democratic candidates. The Republican Party under leaders Mitch McConnell and Kevin McCarthy has clearly not attempted to move toward the center. Congresswoman Liz Cheney, daughter of a Republican vice president, was demoted from a congressional leadership position for objecting to some of Trump's policies. Radical voices such as Matt Gaetz and Margery Taylor Greene are gaining increasing traction among the Republican faithful. Thus, Republicans are left only with the second option: obstruct votes for their opponents.

Donald Trump has led the Republican charge toward the right and toward an anti-democratic society. His core belief system is not about preserving America's system of government, but about winning—by any means necessary. Given his charismatic personality, his dominance and control over other weaker Republicans, and the unbridled support of his fan club, he has run roughshod over traditional American values and morals. Had the courts ruled in his favor after the election, or had the January 6 protests been successful, or had he been able to impose martial law on the country after his defeat, he would have happily reigned over the United States without a thought as to the ruins of democracy.

Having failed to continue in the White House, Trump has resorted to promulgating the big lie every chance he gets. How far the Republican Party will go to appease him and how successful the Democratic Party and "never Trump" Republicans will be in preserving democracy remains to be seen.

> *"More than half of Republicans endorsed a false claim that the attack was 'led by violent leftwing protesters trying to make Trump look bad."*

Political Violence Threatens Democracy

Lois Beckett

In the following viewpoint, Lois Beckett cites polls that show that an estimated fifty million Republicans still believe former president Donald Trump's assertion that he won the 2020 election. A small percentage of Trump's supporters say they would support violence to remedy this problem. Even a small amount of people perpetrating political violence can have devastating, lasting effects on both people and on democracies, if the majority does not stop them. Lois Beckett is a senior reporter for the Guardian.

As you read, consider the following questions:

1. How has the "end" of the COVID-19 pandemic changed the political climate in America?
2. Why do some Trump voters feel abandoned?
3. Is it apt for Jhacova Williams to compare January 6th with lynchings in the American South?

"Millions of Americans Think the Election Was Stolen. How Worried Should We Be About More Violence?" by Lois Beckett, Guardian News and Media Limited, February 16, 2021. Reprinted by permission.

Three months after an insurrection at the US Capitol, an estimated 50 million Republicans still believe the false claim that the 2020 election was stolen from Donald Trump, according to a recent national survey. But it's far from clear how many Americans might still be willing to take violent action in support of that belief.

Early research on the continued risk of violence related to Trump's "big lie" has produced a wide variety of findings. One political scientist at the University of Chicago estimated, based on a single national survey in March, that the current size of an ongoing "insurrectionist movement" in the US might be as large as 4% of American adults, or about 10 million people.

Other experts on political violence cautioned that survey results about what Americans believe provide virtually no insight on how many of them will ever act on those beliefs. Researchers who have interviewed some of Trump's most loyal supporters over the past months say that many of them appear to be cooling down – still believing the election was stolen, but not eager to do much about it. The handful of attempts by far-right extremist groups to mobilize nationwide protests after 6 January have mostly fizzled.

"Lots of people talk the talk, but very few walk the walk," Michael Jensen, a senior researcher who specializes in radicalization at the National Consortium for the Study of Terrorism and Responses to Terrorism (Start), told the Guardian. "Only a tiny fraction of the people who adhere to radical views will act on them."

More than 800 people from a crowd of more than 10,000 are estimated to have breached the Capitol building, the acting Capitol police chief said in February. Nearly 400 of them are now facing charges.

Extremism experts have called the 6 January attack an example of "mass radicalization", with a majority of people charged in the incident having no affiliation with existing extremist groups, according to early analyses. More than half of the people charged in the insurrection appeared to have planned their participation alone, not even coordinating with family members or close friends, according to one analysis. Nearly half were business owners or had white-collar jobs, and very few were unemployed, a sharp contrast with the profiles of some previous violent rightwing extremists.

Today Trump's relative silence and the gradual return to more normal life as more Americans have been vaccinated, have

STILL THINK TRUMP ISN'T A THREAT TO DEMOCRACY?

For the last four years the Courant, along with other newspapers, has warned just how dangerous Donald Trump was, that he cared only about his own power and glory and not a whit for the values that lie at the heart of our Republic.

We've been called snowflakes, nay sayers, bleeding hearts, fake news and anti-American by many of those who support Trump. We've been criticized by local Republicans who have been willing over the last four years to turn a blind eye to the damage Trump was causing in the hopes of riding the president's populist coattails.

We have a simple request for you today: Turn on your television.

Watch as the nation's Capitol building is swarmed by thugs, as the lawful certification of a Democratically-elected president is interrupted by lawless seditionists. Watch as our Democracy—once a beacon to the world—is reduced to a laughing stock.

Please don't lie to yourself. This is an insurrection, a coup. This is an attack on Democracy itself. There are reports at this writing of shots being fired on the Capitol grounds.

The responsibility lies with the president. Any blood shed today is on his hands. Since he lost the election to Democrat Joe Biden, Trump has spewed one lie after another about the election being stolen from him. He has persisted in his claims despite overwhelming evidence that this was a fair and free election.

And, faced with today's final act in Congress to certify the result, Trump upped the ante, fomenting anger and dissent, even attacking his own vice president for doing the job he swore an oath to do. And, now, we see the result: Violence. Terror.

Trump always was dangerous. Today we learned just how dangerous he is.

"Editorial: Still think Donald Trump Isn't a Threat to Democracy? Turn on Your TV," by Hartford Courant, Hartford Courant, January 6, 2021.

created very different conditions than in the days and weeks before 6 January.

"The charismatic leader has been silenced for the most part. He might find his way back into the public spotlight, but as of right now, he's been effectively muted," Jensen said.

"We were in a really unique situation with the pandemic, and the lockdowns, and people being isolated and fearful. You had a vulnerable population," he added. Today, "people are getting back to their lives."

The "Cooling Out"

In the aftermath of the Capitol attack, a large majority of Americans condemned the rioters and said they should be prosecuted.

But research in the past months has also shown that many Republican voters are still loyal to Trump and receptive to lies from him and other Republican politicians about the 2020 election and the insurrection that followed.

A March survey from Reuters/Ipsos found that more than half of Republicans endorsed a false claim that the attack was "led by violent leftwing protesters trying to make Trump look bad", and also said they believed that the people who gathered at the Capitol "were mostly peaceful, law-abiding Americans".

Six in 10 Republicans in that survey also said they believed "the 2020 election was stolen from Donald Trump." That percentage of the sample would correspond with roughly 50 to 55 million Americans, Chris Jackson, the Ipsos senior vice-president for public affairs, told the Guardian.

In mid-March, researchers at the University of Chicago attempted to home in on the percentage of Americans who still believed in Trump's "big lie," and who also may be willing to act violently as a result, using a nationally representative sample of a thousand American adults.

Two-thirds of the respondents said they believed the election was legitimate, the researchers found. Another 27% said they believed the election had been stolen from Trump, but endorsed only non-violent protest. Only 4% said they believed the election was stolen, and also expressed a willingness to engage in violent protest.

That 4% would translate to roughly 10 million American adults, said Robert Pape, a political scientist at the Chicago Project on Security and Threats who specialized in global suicide terror attacks, and who pivoted last year to focus on political violence in the United States.

Other experts have argued that what survey respondents mean when they say they support using violence to achieve their political goals is far from obvious, according to Nathan Kalmoe, a political scientist at Louisiana State University who has been polling Americans about political violence since 2017.

The findings of that research are concerning: as of February, 20% of Republicans and 13% of Democrats now say violence is at least "a little" justified to advance their party's goals.

But only a small fraction of the respondents who had said violence by their side was at least "a little justified" in a previous survey endorsed armed, fatal violence, Kalmoe said, instead mentioning fistfights, property destruction and non-violent actions like insults. "'Violence' doesn't mean mass death or even killing even among the people who think some violence is OK," Kalmoe said.

"There are many steps from attitudes to behavioral intentions to behaviors that stop people from acting violently, even when they hold violent views," he added. Knowing how many people might complete all of those steps was a "nearly impossible question".

Christopher Parker, a political scientist who studies race and the evolution of US rightwing movements, said that a preliminary finding that 4% of American adults believed the election was stolen from Trump and endorsed violence was a plausible survey result, given that about 7% of American adults had said they participated in a Tea Party event.

A March survey by the Pew research center found a similar proportion of Americans expressing the most skeptical view of a crackdown on the Capitol rioters, with 4% saying it was "not at all important" for them to be prosecuted.

But it was also very possible that the attitudes of Trump supporters were shifting over time, Parker cautioned, and that the 4% figure from mid-March may already be shrinking.

In focus groups with Trump loyalists in Wisconsin and Georgia that Parker worked on, Trump supporters appeared "angry, but also despondent, feeling powerless and uncertain they will become more involved in politics." Trump voters appeared to be much less threatened by Biden than they were by Obama, the focus groups indicated, and were interested in what Biden's post-pandemic recovery plan might do for them personally.

Arlie Hochschild, a sociologist who is currently conducting interviews in the region, found that in eastern Kentucky, even among dedicated Trump supporters, there had been a "cooling out."

Hochschild, the author of *Strangers in Their Own Land: Anger and Mourning on the American Right*, said that Trump's most ardent supporters, the ones who believe the election was stolen from him, "are in a squeeze", feeling threatened by the law enforcement crackdown on the Capitol rioters on one hand, and a sense of abandonment at Trump's behavior on the other.

On 6 January, some Trump supporters "had felt proud, patriotic, defending democracy, and in a day's time that had turned around to dishonor, criminalization. They were put down. The law was looking for them," she said. At the same time, "I think a lot of people have felt abandoned. Trump did not pardon [the Capitol rioters]. He went away, disappeared into silence. They feel like: 'Wait a minute: why isn't he speaking up for us? Why isn't he defending us?'"

A minority of Trump supporters Hochschild is interviewing today are doubling down on their election fraud beliefs, she said, expressing paranoia about big government taking over, and feeling "monitored and unsafe." But the majority has "divested emotion from the issue" of "election fraud." Experts cautioned that even the tiniest fraction of people willing to use violence in support of their extreme beliefs is dangerous, particularly in the US, where political violence in recent years has often taken the form of high-casualty mass shootings in places like churches, synagogues and stores.

Hochschild said she is more concerned about further political violence in the long term than the short term. "I do feel there are a lot of people whose position is extreme," she said. "I just don't see it mobilized at this point."

"The reality is, when you see 6 January, that was not a large share of Americans that did that," said Jhacova Williams, a Rand Corporation economist who has studied the after-effects of lynchings in the American south.

Still, she said, political violence can have devastating, lasting effects, on both people and on democracies, while being driven by relatively small numbers of people, as long as the majority does not intervene.

While lynchings were held in public and attracted crowds, "If you look historically, it wasn't as if you had masses in the south that were lynching people," Williams said. "It was a subset of people who were doing that."

> *"Trump's singular achievement is the destruction of the Republican Party party that ... now looks like a reckless organization where racist, homophobic, xenophobic and misogynist views are being normalized."*

Trump Has Made an Ugly Spectacle of Democracy

Salil Tripathi

In the following viewpoint, Salil Tripathi argues that Donald Trump has made a mockery of political norms in the United States. With each word and act, Trump sinks to lower depths, according to the author. He has challenged the results of the 2020 elections, and his supporters in Congress have defended him, hoping to gain the 2024 Republican nomination. While some Republicans have stayed true to the US Constitution, a minority is willing to defy traditional norms for political benefit. All of this puts the United States in a precarious position, argues Tripathi. Salil Tripathi is the chair of PEN International's Writers in Prison Committee. His work has appeared in the Washington Post, *the* New York Times, *and the* New Yorker, *among others.*

"The Ugly Spectacle that Trump Has Turned US Democracy Into," by Salil Tripathi, Livemint, January 6, 2021. Reprinted by permission.

As you read, consider the following questions:

1. This viewpoint was published just before the Capitol riot. How would the events of that day confirm what the author writes?
2. Why has Mike Pence been placed in a difficult position?
3. What facts does the viewpoint present that undermine Trump's popularity?

For a president who plumbs to lower depths with each public utterance, Donald Trump's graceless performance since his electoral defeat in November would surprise nobody. But the manner in which he has tried to subvert institutions is appalling. His lawyers have made unhinged assertions. He has welcomed a disgraced former associate to the White House whose recommendation is for Trump to call in the army. He has tried bullying Georgian officials, by claiming—without any evidence—that the election in that state was flawed, and pleaded that the officials somehow find some 11,000 votes so that he can flip the state in his favour. He has not criticized his supporters who vandalized four African-American churches in Washington.

In a pathetic exercise of grandstanding, a few Republican members of the House of Representatives and about a dozen Republican senators are trying to challenge the electoral college vote, with the sole aim of compelling their saner Republican colleagues to defend the duly-certified electoral college votes, or repudiate those. If the majority of Republican senators ratify the vote for Biden, they run the risk of insurgent pro-Trump challenges when they seek re-election (and five relatively moderate Republicans are particularly vulnerable). If they do repudiate the vote, they unleash the energized Trump supporters they disagree with. The role of a relatively senior senator like Ted Cruz (who ran unsuccessfully for the Republican nomination in 2016) is particularly cynical and galling. He and senator Josh Hawley are fighting against the inevitable not because they believe Trump's alternate view of reality; rather, they seek to inherit the Trump constituency in 2024 for the next presidential race. It places vice-president Mike Pence, a likely candidate in 2024, in a quandary: he must declare the outcome. If he stays loyal to Trump and lets the dispute fester, he throws the constitution overboard; if he acts responsibly, he allows Cruz to become the frontrunner.

The situation is grim enough for ten former secretaries of defense to write a joint appeal calling upon the army to stay out of the electoral process. Dozens of corporate chiefs have urged the US Congress to name Joe Biden as the duly-elected president. It is preposterous even to think that such appeals have become necessary; such shenanigans are common in countries new to democracy, unused to peaceful transfers of power; not in a country that has held elections since the late 18th century, even during world wars and an economic depression. Think of how the US State Department has reacted to presidents in other countries holding on to power after losing elections. Trump is following those presidents, but only up to a point. He hasn't jailed opponents, imposed censorship, or called in the troops yet, but it's hard to argue that's because he cherishes democracy. He probably realizes that the generals will say no. After all, several judges he has appointed at federal courts have thrown out his legal challenges in 60 cases across America, and even the Supreme Court, where he appointed three of the nine judges, has dismissed his fact-free complaints.

Trump's singular achievement is the destruction of the Republican Party. A party that believed in a small government, which was on the right side during the US Civil War, which believed in free trade, and which focused on individual responsibility (against collective obligations), now looks like a reckless organization where racist, homophobic, xenophobic and misogynist views are being normalized. Critics of Republicans would argue that they were always like that, but that's unfair; there have been many constitutionalist and responsible Republicans. The effort to impeach Richard Nixon wasn't partisan.

To be sure, there are Republicans who claim to stand by those values. But a few exceptions apart, many have left it till too late. Establishment Republicans have allowed their party to be stolen; it is now a grotesque caricature of its former self.

Politicians like Cruz assume that America has changed, and humouring an extremist base will yield political dividends. That's not unreasonable. Trump got 74 million votes in November, more votes than any candidate in American political history except Biden, who won 81 million votes. Trump got 11 million more votes than his 2016 tally (when his rival that year, Hillary Clinton, had outpolled him by 3 million votes but lost the US electoral college). Biden not only won more votes, he won key states, to win the electoral college 306-232. Trump is popular, but we should remember that in neither 2016 nor 2020 did he win the majority of votes.

Cruz's embrace of extremism could destroy moderates. If Trump does not run in 2024 (he will be 78, which is Biden's age now), and doesn't anoint a successor (his daughter Ivanka, for example), or is mired in lawsuits, his constituency is up for grabs. That's what Cruz, Pence and others want.

American institutions have held firm so far, but they have been shaken at the core. America needs to safeguard its constitution. The law will catch up with citizen Trump; but he has eroded and undermined norms, and recovering what's lost will be hard.

> "This signals the extent to which our politics have become polarized. … The onus, then, increasingly lies on politicians, whose words wield even more power when their followers closely identify with them."

Voters Are Starting to Act Like Sports Fanatics

Michael Devlin and Natalie Brown Devlin

In the following viewpoint, Michael Devlin and Natalie Brown Devlin pose the question of how American politics arrived at the point where there were essentially two "teams," the red (conservative) and the blue (liberal). The authors label this development "political fandom," pointing to highly identified fans, whose lives and psyches are so intertwined with their teams that losses are personal and devastating. The Devlins suggest that it is up to politicians to accept reality, lose graciously, and not inflame their highly identified political base. Michael Devlin is an associate professor of communication at Texas State University. Natalie Brown Devlin is an ssistant professor of advertising at the University of Texas at Austin.

As you read, consider the following questions:

1. What parallels do the authors draw between sports and politics?
2. What excuses do highly identified fans make when their team loses?
3. What impact does a losing athlete's acceptance or rejection of a loss have on fans of the losing team?

During Donald Trump's presidency, the American electorate became more divided and partisan, with research suggesting that the ongoing division is less about policy and more about labels like "conservative" and "liberal."

Essentially, voters increasingly see themselves in one of two camps—a "red team" and "blue team," each with a faction of hard-core members.

The dangerous extent of this devotion was on display when a mob of Trump supporters stormed the US Capitol, convinced that the election had been stolen despite no credible evidence of widespread voter fraud.

How did American politics get to this point?

As sports communication researchers who have written extensively on the vast and powerful influence of identity on attitudes and behavior, we believe our work can offer some ways to understand recent events.

We've noted parallels between political identity and sports fandom that, when unpacked, point to some of the dangers associated with what we call "political fandom."

Fandom Can Be Central to Identity

In sports, the spectrum of fandom is easily observable. Some fans might casually enjoy games simply while wearing their team's shirt, whereas others ardently support and uproariously react to every play while cloaked in elaborate, outlandish outfits.

But fandom can go beyond outfits. It can become a core component of your identity—your sense of who you are.

Sports communication researchers refer to this connection as "team identification," a concept that transcends simply supporting a team and is, instead, characterized by a deeper, emotional attachment in which fans feel psychologically connected to their favorite team.

These fans—called "highly identified fans"—are more likely to express their love of their team on social media, attend events and consume more team-related media. They'll even buy team-related products when they don't particularly like the product itself. For the fan, it's all about demonstrating allegiance.

Research shows that being a fan and belonging to a group can be beneficial to someone's well-being. But there can be a darker side to this kind of devoted fandom—particularly when a favorite team loses.

Wins and Losses Become Personal

In sports, the final whistle signals a game's end.

But the level to which fans identify with their team can actually influence how they feel and act after the game has been decided. For highly identified fans, a win feels like a personal victory; a loss, on the other hand, feels like a personal defeat.

After wins, highly identified fans are more likely to bask in the glory of victory, tying themselves to the team through the use of language like "us" and "we."

For those same highly identified fans, a loss isn't simply disappointing. Instead, it poses a threat to their identity and causes psychological discomfort that leads to stress, depression and a greater willingness to confront others. They'll often double down in support of their team. They might declare their team the best, regardless of the outcome. They'll say the loss was a fluke and that external causes were to blame—poor officiating, an injury or cheating by the other team.

As with sports, political identification and participation can occur on a spectrum. Some people simply vote every election cycle for their preferred political party. Others, however, are heavily invested in the party and its candidates. They devour media, purchase campaign-affiliated merchandise and frequently flaunt their support in public and on social media.

After the 2020 presidential election, we wanted to know to what extent the concept of team identification applied to politics. We surveyed voters between Dec. 16 and Dec. 20, 2020, just days after the Electoral College vote confirmed Joe Biden as president-elect. Administering a questionnaire that's used by sport communication researchers, we were able to show "team identification"—when applied to politics—can help explain certain beliefs and behaviors after the election.

We found that 55% of Trump voters in our survey still falsely believed that Donald Trump had won the 2020 election. This result was significantly influenced by their level of team identification; voters who were highly identified Trump supporters were more likely to hold this false belief.

Of course, Trump, some members of Congress and conservative media outlets reinforced those false beliefs by sharing baseless information alleging election irregularities and voter fraud.

When we asked highly identified Trump supporters if they were likely to distance themselves after the loss, we found they retained unfettered loyalty to Trump, similar to the way a sports fan would react after a big loss. When asked why Biden had been declared president-elect, overwhelmingly, they blamed everything but Trump, most often echoing Trump's false voter fraud claims.

The Ball Is in the Politician's Court

This issue, however, is not unique to Trump and his supporters.

Many politicians have devoted fans. Our results showed—perhaps surprisingly—that both Biden and Trump voters rated similarly in terms of their levels of political team identification.

To us, this signals the extent to which our politics have become polarized, with voters existing in separate camps that are unflaggingly devoted to their "team" and its leaders.

The onus, then, increasingly lies on politicians, whose words wield even more power when their followers closely identify with them.

In sports, after losing a close playoff game, a star player can congratulate the other team and admit to being outplayed or can blame the refs and accuse the other side of cheating without offering evidence. The former reaction might temper the emotions of die-hard fans, while the latter could easily exacerbate their negative feelings.

It's important for political leaders to consider the influence of political fandom. After an election, conceding after the "final whistle has blown" is an important norm and tradition, while divisive rhetoric that fans the flames of false hope is a dangerous tack to take. After all, in sports, highly identified fans are much more likely to become aggressive when they expect their team to win, only to witness a loss.

Politics, though, isn't a game. And on Jan. 6, the world saw what happens when political fandom is harnessed and unleashed by unfounded, inflammatory rhetoric.

> "*This moment is ripe for just about anything: The dawn of new conspiracy subcultures, so-called 'blackpilling' (when radicalized people turn to far-right and white supremacist beliefs), and, of course, individual acts of domestic terror.*"

Trump's Losses Leave His Diehard Fans Adrift

Anna Merlan and Mack Lamoureux

In the following viewpoint, Anna Merlan and Mack Lamoureux argue that hardcore Trump fans believed that Trump would ascend to the role of "God-Emperor," thereby establishing his iron grip over the United States and, effectively, ending American democracy. When Biden was inaugurated and Trump ascended not to a throne, but to the aircraft that would take him to his Florida compound, his truest fans were devastated. They believed that they no longer had a sitting president and awaited further orders from their leader. Anna Merlan writes for Vice and specializes in subcultures, alternative communities, conspiracy theories, crime, belief, death, sexual violence. and women's lives. Mack Lamoureux writes for Vice, among other outlets.

"Trump Fails to Ascend as God Emperor, Leaving Diehard Fans Adrift," by Anna Merlan and Mack Lamoureux, Vice News, January 21, 2021. Reprinted by permission.

As you read, consider the following questions:

1. Which online platforms do Trump supporters frequent?
2. What is "blackpilling"?
3. Why are some Trump supporters still hopeful?

A s new President Joseph R. Biden took his oath of office, his hand atop a massive family Bible, confusion, anger, and grief washed over some of the worst corners of the Internet. Refugees from the QAnon conspiracy subreddit, now huddled together on a new website, took turns assuring each other that everything they were seeing was all part of the unfolding of the grand Plan they'd spent years breathlessly awaiting. "I HAVE ZERO DOUBTS," one wrote. But others weren't so sure. "WTF?," another wrote. "He's being sworn in now."

"Anyone else," another wrote, "feeling beyond let down right now?"

In the weeks leading up to Biden's inauguration, the worst elements of Trump's coalition—Nazis, white supremacists, Q-mesmerized "patriots," Proud Boys, Telegram lurkers, and all-purpose far-right s---tlords—managed to hold out hope. On one website for Trump fans banished from Reddit, TheDonald.win, many users had assured one another that not only would Biden never take office, but that Trump, naturally, would never leave it. Instead, they claimed to each other—in a refrain that was once ironic and seemed less so all the time—that he would ascend to the role of "God Emperor." On the morning of January 20, QAnon fans urged each other to "Enjoy the show," dotting their posts with popcorn emojis, meant to symbolize all of them sitting back and watching Armageddon rain down on the Satanic cabal they'd been led to believe rules the world.

Instead, Trump quietly boarded a helicopter and flew away, Biden was sworn in without a hitch, and these increasingly addled and radicalized people were left to turn on each other.

"I have to say I am amazed that there's not even a single protest going on," one TheDonald.win user wrote. "Honestly we really are the cucks in the end. Sat back and watched it all happen."

Users on MeWe, a Facebook alternative to which many far-right users have decamped, mourned the victory of Satan and posted impassioned screeds.

"The Biggest Fraud In American History... It's A Disgrace To The Constitution America And GOD," one user wrote. "Thou Shall Not Steal... This My First And Last Post To This Abomination Of Justice."

This is a bizarre, dangerous, and volatile moment for Trump's most impassioned and hateful fans. They have been forced to recognize that the glorious reckoning they dreamed of would not come to pass, that Trump would not and will not usher in either— take your pick—God's kingdom on earth or a white ethnostate. And in that moment, these people are vulnerable to any new bad idea that comes along.

On Telegram, the .win sites, and the other corners of the internet where people have gathered in the wake of a mass ejection from the major social-media sites, they are declaring they no longer believe in anything. This moment is ripe for just about anything: The dawn of new conspiracy subcultures, so-called "blackpilling" (when radicalized people turn to far-right and white supremacist beliefs), and, of course, individual acts of domestic terror.

One of the pinned tweets on a large QAnon forum reminds Q adherents that it's important to "take care of your mental health today." A great majority of the users on the site seem despondent and directionless. At least one group, the Proud Boys, has seized upon the void Trump's departure has left in his followers' lives. On one of their official channels on Telegram they tell Trump fans "here is hope. Not for Trump to become president, but there is hope for our future. Abandon the GOP. Embrace the ultranationalist 3rd position."

(Gavin McInnes was a co-founder of VICE. He left the company in 2008 and has had no involvement since then. He later founded the Proud Boys in 2016. McInnes says he left the Proud Boys in 2018.)

On InfoWars, Alex Jones—for whom the Trump era represented both a glorious rise and equally precipitous fall—seemed subdued. For commentary, he brought on Elmer Stewart Rhodes, the founder of the Oath Keepers, who appeared sitting in his car, shot from below at the most unflattering possible angle, apparently on his cellphone. "We no longer have a legitimate sitting president," Rhodes told Jones, who nodded, grimly.

Moments later, Jones, sounding especially hoarse, pivoted joylessly to one of his signature supplement ads. "With all these pressures, you need a high quality multivitamin," he told his audience tonelessly.

Not all are despondent, however. Some are already thrilled by the idea that Trump is apparently speculating about forming a Patriot Party. A few actually started a Patriot Party website, which is built around "small government, America First, and Big Freedom." They await further instruction from their leader.

"Party and website are both works in progress," reads the fine print at the bottom of the website. "Please stay tuned."

"I think we underestimate the way that Trump can help determine the future of American politics through the party system."

Trump Damaged American Democracy

Brendan Nyhan and Matt Grossman

In the following excerpted interview, Matt Grossman poses questions concerning US democracy to Brendan Nyhan. While Nyhan suggests that Trump has done harm to American democratic institutions, much of his extreme behavior was rhetorical and not legislative. He governed as a conservative Republican, lowering taxes and installing conservative judges. But rhetoric can do damage, Nyhan states, and Trump's language has been dangerous. While it is true that traditional norms have held when it came to preserving democracy, the future is in doubt. Trump has presided over a period of destabilization in America, and it will not be easy to right the ship of state. Matt Grossmann is director of the Institute for Public Policy and Social Research and a professor of political science at Michigan State University. Brendan Nyhan is a professor in the department of government at Dartmouth College.

"How Much Did Trump Undermine US Democracy?" by Brendan Nyhan, Niskanen Center, December 30, 2020. https://www.niskanencenter.org/how-much-did-trump-undermine-u-s-democracy/. Licensed under CC by 4.0 International.

As you read, consider the following questions:

1. What are some specific examples of traditional norms that President Trump has violated?
2. In what sense, according to the authors, did America get lucky?
3. What fears does Nyhan have about the Democratic Party's response to Trump?

W ill Trump do lasting damage to American democratic institutions? He has repeatedly broken norms during his presidency and tried to overturn the results of the 2020 election. How much is the US undergoing democratic backsliding and what did his presidency reveal about the strength and limits of our institutions? Brendan Nyhan is an organizer of Bright Line Watch, an effort to survey experts and the public to track the erosion of democratic norms under Trump. He finds significant signs of weakness but acknowledges the many future unknowns. In this special year-end conversational edition, we review the damage and the evidence. Transcript:

Matt Grossmann: How much did Trump undermine American democracy for good, this week on The Science of Politics. For the Niskanen Center, I'm Matt Grossmann. Donald Trump has broken democratic norms throughout his presidency in words and deeds, and tried to impede and overturn the results of the 2020 election. How much significant democratic backsliding did he create? And what did his presidency reveal about the strength and limits of our institutions? This week, I'm joined by Brendan Nyhan of Dartmouth and The Upshot for a special conversational edition. He's an organizer of Bright Line Watch, an effort to survey experts and the public about American democratic norms, tracking their erosion. He finds significant signs of weakness, many of which are likely to last. I have an ever-so-slightly more optimistic view, so you'll hear me interject more than usual. Here's our conversation, which also offers a bit of 2020 year in review and post-election retrospective.

Bright Line Watch has been going for 13 waves of expert surveys and 11 waves of the public surveys. What are the biggest things you've learned and the biggest surprises?

Brendan Nyhan: Well, we've learned a lot about the state of US democracy, both the good news and the bad news. I think we're really proud of the data that we've been able to put together tracking the status of US democracy over this time period. We've never had such high-frequency data, both in terms of perceptions of US democracy among the public, and perceptions of US democracy among political science experts too. So I think that's an important resource. And it's given us an anchor. There's no objective measurable way to directly assess democracy as such, how well is it working? But we think it gives an important window into how things have developed during the Trump presidency. So we're very proud of that.

I think what I've learned from it is just how multidimensional democracy is in the fullest sense. The full idea of liberal democracy that has this bundle that includes the rule of law, constraints on the use of power, and the exercise of influence by the public at the ballot box and through public opinion's effect on elected representatives and so forth, that full bundle is quite complex. And thinking about its status is not an easy thing. So it's been really helpful to me to disaggregate that and to think about all these different aspects. And then when we talk about the state of US democracy, to be specific, do we think US democracy is improving or worsening? And if so, in what areas?In what ways? And so I think we've been able to be more precise about that.

Matt Grossmann: So it sounds like you started thinking that there were bright lines that we might cross or not cross, but ended up thinking that it was a lot more complicated than a clear line. So talk about how this developed and where you think you succeeded and failed.

Brendan Nyhan: Yeah. I don't want to say that we haven't crossed any bright lines, because we've crossed a lot more lines than I thought were possible to cross. I guess that's a bit convoluted. But I'm struck by how much has happened since we started this project in early 2017. It's been a long process. What the Bright Line Watch helps us do is to see how far we've come. So we clearly started it because we were worried about the state of US democracy after what we saw during the 2016 campaign. President Trump, then candidate Trump, repeatedly violated norms as a candidate in a way we hadn't seen before in modern American political history. Bright Line Watch was started by my colleagues, Sue Stokes at The University of Chicago, Gretchen Helmke at the University of Rochester, and my colleague here at Dartmouth, John Kerry. I later joined the project to track the state of US democracy, given that President Trump had won and would be entering office.

So I think we've been successful at documenting just how far we've come, and how many lines have been crossed, and in what areas. So we can now see with the benefit of hindsight not just that experts think US democracy has declined since President Trump entered as a candidate and then took office, but we've seen in particular the areas in which they think US democracy has declined. In particular, judicial constraints on the executive, legislative constraints on the executive, Constitutional constraints on the executive, toleration of protest, and refraining from using government agencies to punish your political opponents. So those are important principles of democracy. They're not the only ones, but those are the ones that really stand out over time as areas where experts have identified deterioration that we've seen during the time that we've been tracking the Trump administration.

Matt Grossmann: So, yeah. Let's do an exercise where we talk about the most alarming, the least alarming, both in the types of lines, but also in the characterization of the story. So let's start out with the most alarmist possible version of the story. Where are the clear cases where Donald Trump has violated democratic norms and undermined democracy in the US that stand the most chance of lasting?

Brendan Nyhan: I think his ongoing attack on the peaceful transfer of power is the most obvious and important case. Our experts rate it as the most important of the highly abnormal acts that have taken place during the Trump presidency. The peaceful transfer of power is central to democracy itself. Trump has refused to accept the legitimacy of his defeat. He's encouraging his followers to view the election as illegitimate. He's scheming ways to overturn the election result. And he's encouraging a generation of Republican elected officials to emulate these tactics in the future, which I think could be incredibly destructive even if he leaves the political scene after this election, which doesn't appear to be likely. But at some point, he will leave.

His legacy, though, could be calling into question something that had never been called into question in my lifetime. High-ranking officials in the military have to disavow the prospect of them becoming involved in determining the outcome of an American election. No one does that in Denmark. No one does that in stable, consolidated democracies. The fact that the military has to say, "No. We're not involved in determining who wins this election," is itself a profound violation of democratic norms. Similarly, the president holding an election where … Declaring martial law or seizing voting machines is being contemplated, and is a profound violation of democratic norms, an infraction which should lead to the immediate impeachment and removal from office of any president who contemplates using martial law to overturn the results of an election.

So I think this whole series of events is incredibly alarming. Trump will not succeed. Joe Biden will be sworn in on January 20th. But it has expanded the set of possibilities and destabilized the expectations around the peaceful transfer of power in a way that I think is quite corrosive.

Matt Grossmann: Those sound pretty Trump-specific, though. I mean, is it he could inspire generations, but they might also see it as a long, failed effort that looks foolish in retrospect? So what are the biggest signs that these are permanent shifts? Is it just that the actions are norm-breaking and norm-creating? Or have there been real changes to our institutions that are likely to be permanent?

Brendan Nyhan: This is the paradox of Trump. Most of his norm violations are rhetorical and not institutional. So we have to decide how much they matter. It's very much a fair point to say that Donald Trump didn't accomplish very much when it came to policy. And most of what he did accomplish was conventional Republican policy or political goals, like cutting taxes and installing conservative judges. In an institutional sense, he was often a very conventional Republican president. But these rhetorical acts are not without meaning and substance. He has established a hold over the Republican Party that is going to shape the incentives of elected officials going forward. It's going to provide an important signal to those ambitious politicians who want to hold and achieve power that this is the way to inspire support and loyalty from their base.

I think we underestimate the way that Trump can help determine the future of American politics through the party system. It's not the same as changing institutional rules or policies in the short term. But if he's changing the character of the Republican Party in the short to medium term, that's incredibly important. Who's going to run for secretary of state in Republican primaries in battleground states in the future? And who's going to be nominated coming out of those races? Who's going to win primaries? There's a candidate running in Virginia right now for governor who says that Trump should declare martial law. Now, she appears to be such a fringe candidate that hopefully she'll be defeated. But there will be more candidates like that, and there will be more people like that. I worry that we're starting to see Pandora's box open as other candidates respond to the demand for these kinds of illiberalism that Trump has helped to unleash.

Matt Grossmann: So another way of seeing it is that our institutions just got a long series of very tough tests. And the courts and Congress and state institutions and all of that did push back in some cases. So talk to me about that case for a little bit. What would be the best case you could make that our institutions showed their strength, despite the threat from Trump?

Brendan Nyhan: No, that's right. And it's an important piece of the story too. We need to be judicious. The threat is real, but the areas of strength are important to highlight as well. Conservative judges turned back Trump's appeals, not just liberal ones. His efforts to overturn the election were laughed out of court basically across the board, regardless of the background of the judges. That's a really encouraging sign. The local and state election officials who carried off a remarkably successful election during this pandemic are real heroes of the republic. That's an incredible area of strength. And I think the military has to a large extent held the line against Trump, and resisted being drawn into political controversies or being used in ways that Trump might like it to be used as a kind of political prop or instrument for his agenda.

But I guess what I would say is these institutions will start to buckle under strain if the pressure on them is not alleviated. The local and state elections, the people who get involved in those, if they face death threats, will leave, the good ones. The bad ones will start to run. If the military becomes politicized, who gets promoted within the military? Those norms around civil-military relations may deteriorate. We saw this with the Department of Justice, which at first held the line to some extent under Trump. But once Bill Barr was there and was able to start more effectively maneuvering the instruments of power, we saw more and more violations of norms and previously standard procedures there than we'd seen before.

So I think there are these real areas of strength. But they're not infinitely durable. They won't necessarily hold up if this pressure continues. We can potentially turn the page. But we shouldn't assume they will indefinitely be able to sustain this kind of pressure.

THE DARKEST HOUR

In shocking scenes without precedent in US politics, pro-Trump rioters stormed the US Capitol as Congress was meeting to ceremonially certify the Electoral College votes and confirm Joe Biden as the next US president. Four people have reportedly died as rioters fought with law enforcement forces, scaled the walls of the Capitol building, vandalised government property and disrupted Congress proceedings. President Donald Trump cannot disavow his role in fomenting this chaos. For weeks after losing the presidential polls in November, he has put out a stream of falsehoods claiming victory and alleging widespread electoral fraud. He has been deliberately exciting his base of radical right-wing followers, with the aim of overturning the election result. It's hard to describe this as anything short of an attempted coup.

That such scenes should play out in the world's most powerful democracy, in terms of both hard and soft power, is surely bad news for democracies everywhere. Naturally it has caused shock among world capitals, while the Chinese Communist Party has been handed an unexpected propaganda coup. Prime Minister Narendra Modi has done well to quickly condemn the violence, stating that "democratic process cannot be subverted through unlawful protests".

Matt Grossmann: Talk a little bit more broadly about the bad signs and the good signs during the administration. What did Trump try to do during his administration, beyond, set it up so that he could win the next election or overturn it? And where was he successful? And where were our institutions more strong in keeping it at bay?

Brendan Nyhan: Yeah. So besides the attack on the election results, I think the next-most important event according to our experts was the effort to use the president's power, his executive power against Joe Biden via pressuring Ukraine to investigate him. That was rated as almost as serious a threat to democracy as the effort to overturn the election by our experts. So I think that's a important moment. Our institutions held up in the sense that whistleblowers

Thankfully, saner voices in the Republican Party are prevailing, with Senate majority leader Mitch McConnell and Vice-President Mike Pence condemning the subversion of democratic process. Despite his hectoring officials across US systems—cutting across party lines and including Republican appointed judges in courts— stood up to Trump's falsehoods and called him out. While this attests to the strength of America's democratic institutions and convictions, it must also be noted that this one went down to the wire. And that is bound to diminish America in the world's eyes, while being a source of comfort to authoritarian leaders like President Xi Jinping.

The good news is that Democrats are on course to secure a trifecta—the presidency, house and Senate majority after the run-off results in Georgia. They should get down to reforming the US electoral system so that its processes can't be questioned or challenged in the manner Trump just did. That's the only way to undo the damage to America's prestige and standing in the world caused by this disgraceful course of events. As of now Pence should invoke the 25th Amendment, declare Trump unfit, and remove him from office forthwith.

"The Darkest Hour: Trump's Politics Has Done Great Damage to the Cause of Democracy Around the World," TOI Editorial, January 8, 2021.

revealed Trump's actions and he was impeached, but he was not removed from office. Only one senator was willing to cross party lines to vote to remove him from office. So I'm not sure how much we should take away from that in terms of positive signs. The president has also attacked the media on an ongoing basis. That hasn't taken any particularly solid form.

I mean, Matt, the question I think we should ask is how much should we congratulate ourselves that the president isn't locking up journalists? He's calling them the enemy of the people. Our institutions held in the sense that he's not throwing journalists in jail, but that's not the sort of thing that liberal democracies typically congratulate themselves for doing. So I'm not really sure how much we should see all of these things as victories. He's said many illiberal things. There's a very long list. Most of them he did not act on. So there was a way in which the bureaucracy sort of ignored many of the president's statements. That's a kind of victory, I suppose. But I do think it's still corrosive that those claims are being made.

I also worry, actually, about the damage that's done when the president is saying to do things, and unelected officials decide that it's important to ignore them. In this case, given the illiberalism of the actions that are being called for, it's understandable. But I think we should worry about the idea of, for instance, the military deciding that it gets to decide which civilian dictates it should listen to. That's, again, not a especially healthy development for a democracy.

Matt Grossmann: What about the opposition party? It seems like there was not exactly the one-upsmanship that some feared in anti-democratic actions. As you say, the opposition party impeached the president, tried its hardest to get allies in the president's party. How should we evaluate that?

Brendan Nyhan: I'm not certain. I think it's fair to question the sometimes crude ways that Democrats talked about the Russia investigation, as if it would be a kind of Scooby-Doo confession of a collusion plot. There were certainly conspiracy theories offered that went beyond the available evidence and that were never corroborated. With Democrats, I worry more about the future. I think there's a possibility of a kind of escalating series of Constitutional hardball tactics being deployed against each other by the two parties in a way that could be destabilizing. We might have seen that if Joe Biden and the Democrats had won a landslide, for instance, and there was more momentum to do things like expand the size of the Supreme Court that would be more aggressive forms of Constitutional hardball.

It doesn't seem like those things are in the cards now. But they do seem to have greater prospects on the Democratic side than they once did. There's an argument for Constitutional hardball as a response to norm violations. But there's also a way in which it can be destabilizing. I think that's why it's often split experts when they've debated the merits of those kinds of tactics as a response to violations of democratic norms.

Matt Grossmann: One reading of the post-election period is that we just got lucky. If it came down to only one very close state, then it might have turned out differently. There's been talk about if there was one different judge in Wisconsin, maybe that verdict would have turned out differently. I guess the counter-case is that you don't really know much, you don't observe much about what would have happened in that case from seeing some dissents that aren't going to go into effect. How would you read it? How close did we come? And how much is this dependent on these accidents of history?

Brendan Nyhan: It's a good question. I'm not someone who thinks that Trump would have been successful, necessarily, in overturning the election if it had come down to one state. But I think we have reason to worry that the effort to overturn the election could have become much more serious and destabilizing in that circumstance. We saw almost 2/3 of the House Republican Caucus sign onto the Texas lawsuit, even under the circumstances when it had almost no chance of overturning the result. And we've seen many Republican officials back this effort even though the chances of success were very low, and the legal arguments were considered preposterous.

Matt Grossmann: Doesn't that even if work both ways? I mean, you say it's even if. But that might be because of. That is, this was a fairly costless action at the moment. We might not be able to conclude from that that they would have done it in a circumstance in which it might have been more destabilizing.

[…]

Periodical and Internet Sources Bibliography

The following articles have been selected to supplement the diverse views presented in this chapter.

Madeleine Albright and Michael Chertoff, "Trump's behavior is threat to America's democracy," *USA Today*. December 14, 2020. https://www.usatoday.com/story/opinion/2020/12/14/trumps-behavior-threatens-american-democracy-albright-chertoff-column/6508765002/.

Julia Azari, "Democratic Values Are Still Under Attack — Even Without Trump In The White House," FiveThirtyEight, April 12, 2021. https://fivethirtyeight.com/features/democratic-values-are-still-under-attack-even-without-trump-in-the-white-house/.

Jonathan Bernstein, "Are Republicans Really a Threat to Democracy?" Bloomberg. June 2, 2021. https://www.bloomberg.com/opinion/articles/2021-06-02/are-republicans-really-a-threat-to-democracy.

Phil Boas, "There is no crisis. Trump is no threat to democracy in Arizona or the US," *Arizona Republic*. December 15, 2020. https://www.azcentral.com/story/opinion/op-ed/philboas/2020/12/15/donald-trump-no-threat-democracy-arizona-u-s/3910447001/.

Max Boot, "Opinion: Trump is the worst threat to our democracy since the 1930s," *Washington Post*. September 24, 2020. https://www.washingtonpost.com/opinions/2020/09/24/trump-is-worst-threat-our-democracy-since-1930s/.

Dawn Brancati, "Trump is not the threat to Democracy some claim," *Baltimore Sun*." November 25, 2018. https://www.baltimoresun.com/opinion/op-ed/bs-ed-op-1126-trump-democracy-20181119-story.html.

Uri Friedman, "Democrats Have Found Their Battle Cry," *Atlantic*, July 5, 2019. https://www.theatlantic.com/politics/archive/2019/07/democrats-have-found-their-battle-cry/593881/.

Daniel Henniger, "Who's a Threat to 'Our Democracy'?" *Wall Street Journal*. February 10, 2021. https://www.wsj.com/articles/whos-a-threat-to-our-democracy-11612998812.

Ed Kilgore, "Trump's Delegitimization of Democracy Isn't Wearing Off," *New York*. May 2, 2011. https://nymag.com/intelligencer/2021/05/trumps-delegitimization-of-democracy-isnt-wearing-off.html.

Ezra Klein, "American democracy has faced worse threats than Donald Trump," Vox, May 10, 2018. https://www.vox.com/2018/5/10/17147338/donald-trump-illiberal-undemocratic-elections-politics.

Yascha Mounk, "Is Donald Trump a Danger to Democracy?" *New York Times*, June 18, 2020. https://www.nytimes.com/2020/06/18/books/review/masha-gessen-surviving-autocracy-eric-posner-the-demagogues-playbook.html.

Pippa Norris, "American democracy is at risk from Trump and the Republicans. What can be done?" *Guardian*, June 6, 2021. https://www.theguardian.com/commentisfree/2021/jun/06/republican-party-donald-trump-american-democracy-elections.

Mark Vargas, "Trump isn't the threat to democracy, Democrats are," *Washington Examiner*, September 30, 2019, https://www.washingtonexaminer.com/opinion/trump-isnt-the-threat-to-democracy-democrats-are.

Peter Wehner, "The GOP Is a Grave Threat to American Democracy," *Atlantic*, April 26, 2021. https://www.theatlantic.com/ideas/archive/2021/04/gop-grave-threat-american-democracy/618693/

OPPOSING
VIEWPOINTS®
SERIES

CHAPTER 4

What Is the Future of the Republican Party?

Chapter Preface

To understand the current Republican Party, now firmly in the grasp of Donald J. Trump, one must understand its past, particularly its evolution—many would say radicalization—over forty years from 1980 to 2020. The movement toward modern conservative politics may be said to have begun with Ronald Reagan in 1980 (Some would go farther back to presidential candidate Barry Goldwater, but Goldwater was defeated). After Richard Nixon's resignation in 1973 due to the Watergate scandal, the party had lost its footing in the mid-1970s. But a combination of factors during the Carter administration—double digit inflation and a sense of pessimism about the country in general—led to the rise of Reagan, who rode the optimistic slogan "Morning in America" to victory. Reagan served as president for two terms and was followed by his vice president, George H. W. Bush, in 1988.

Bush was replaced by Democrat Bill Clinton in 1992, but the Republican revolution was only just getting started. Led by firebrand congressman Newt Gingrich, the Republicans retook the House of Representatives during Clinton's first midterm elections in 1994. Gingrich and his followers had no interest in bipartisanship or compromise. Their chief goal was to monitor Clinton's presidency and the chief executive's crimes, specifically his affair with a White House staffer, Monica Lewinsky, worked in Gingrich's favor, as Clinton was impeached by the Republican house.

A third revolutionary moment that furthered the radicalization of the Republican party occurred after the election of Barack Obama in 2008. The Tea Party that emerged during Obama's first term was a populist movement that sought to drive the elites from Washington, lower taxes, and promote traditional American values. Many believe that the Tea Party was an organic, grassroots movement, but it was more likely "astroturfed," that is, organized and seeded with money by billionaire Republican donors. Among these powerful Republican supporters were the Koch Brothers,

Charles and David; Sheldon Adelson, who would, with his wife, go on to be Donald Trump's largest donors; and Australian born businessman Rupert Murdoch, owner of News Corp, the parent company of Fox News. The emergence of right wing media personalities such as Rush Limbaugh and Sean Hannity also helped to fuel the movement.

Donald Trump latched onto this anti-Obama energy, involving himself in the birther conspiracy, which claimed, falsely, that Obama was not born in the United States and was therefore not a legitimate President. When he announced his candidacy for president in 2015, few thought it was anything more than a publicity stunt. A year and a half later he was elected president of the United States.

Since his inauguration in 2017, Trump has strengthened his grasp on the Republican Party. One of his most vocal antagonists in the party, former Republican presidential nominee Mitt Romney said after Trump's defeat in 2020, "He seems to have a pretty good hold on the base of our party. I think that's unlikely to be swayed by almost anything." Trump has facilitated, if not driven the Republican move toward radicalization. As Jackie Calmes writes in the *Los Angeles Times*, "He took ownership of the party's base, and gave license to its racists, conspiracists, zealots and even self-styled paramilitaries, but that base had been calling the shots in the Republican Party for some years, spurred by conservative media."

These groups will move on with or without Trump. The more traditional Republicans, including the "never Trump" contingent, seem powerless against these forces. The two camps are in a pitched battle for the soul of the Republican party, and, given the direction of the party over the last forty years, the old school Republicans don't seem to stand a chance. Time will tell.

> *"Polished populists take a
> different approach, arguing for
> the same policies that Trump
> did ... but without his overtly
> antagonistic language."*

"Polished Populism" May Dominate the Republican Party

David C. Barker and Morgan Marietta

In the following viewpoint David C. Barker and Morgan Marietta discuss a shift in Republican politics away from the crassness of President Trump to a more polished and sanitized version of populism. The core strategies—limiting immigration, opposing "woke" policies, and America first—are still viable, but the harshness of Trump's rhetoric should be stripped away for Republicans to woo those who were turned off by locker room insults. Despite all of Trump's missteps, he remains a popular figure in American politics. Those in the Republican Party who can harness his message without the vitriol may be successful going forward. David C. Barker is a professor of government and director of the Center for Congressional and Presidential Studies at the American University School of Public Affairs. Morgan Marietta is an associate professor of political science at the University of Massachusetts Lowell.

"A Less Trumpy Version of Trumpism Might Be the Future of the Republican Party," by David C. Barker, The Conversation. February 26, 2021. https://theconversation.com/a-less-trumpy-version-of-trumpism-might-be-the-future-of the republican-party-150820. Licensed under CC BY-ND 4.0 International.

As you read, consider the following questions:

1. How do the authors define "populism"?
2. How is populism distinguished from traditional conservatism?
3. Going forward, which Republicans may be able to succeed using polished populism?

Donald Trump lost the 2020 election, but his populist ideas may continue to animate the Republican Party.

As scholars of American beliefs and elections, we can envision a less Trumpy version of Trumpism holding sway over the party in coming years. We call it "polished populism."

Populism is folk-politics based on the premise that ordinary citizens are wiser and more virtuous than supposedly corrupt and self-serving elites. Populist rhetoric is often expressed in cruder, coarser language than ordinary political speech—less like a politician on a stage and more like a guy in a bar.

Trump, a prime practitioner of populist rhetoric, took this to an extreme with the shorthand of Twitter and the insults of the locker room.

Polished populists take a different approach, arguing for the same policies that Trump did—limiting immigration, redistributing wealth toward the working class rather than just the poor, opposing the woke policies of social justice movements, promoting "America First" foreign and trade policies—but without his overtly antagonistic language.

Some Republicans are now arguing for a rejection of populism and a return to traditional conservatism. Those long-standing GOP priorities include limited government, strong national defense of American interests abroad, religious values and, perhaps most importantly, ordinary political personalities.

For two reasons—the GOP's narrow electoral defeat in 2020 and the changing demographics of the Republican Party—we believe that populist policies, if not rhetoric, will continue to be a dominant theme of the Republican Party.

Populism Versus Traditional Conservatism

The contemporary conservatism associated with Ronald Reagan in the 1980s and George W. Bush in the 2000s has several facets and factions, but it can be summed up in the phrase, "You keep what you earn, it's a dangerous world, and God is good."

The economic, national defense and social conservatives of previous decades tended to agree that human nature is untrustworthy and society is fragile, so the US needs to defend against external enemies and internal decline.

IT'S NOT OVER

Donald Trump is reportedly considering replacing Mike Pence as his running mate with a black person or a woman, should he choose to run for president again in 2024.

He believes campaigning with a more diverse potential vice president by his side will stand him in good stead for another run at the White House.

Mike Pence, who appeared to turn on Trump following his election defeat at the hands of Joe Biden, and particularly in the wake of the Capitol riots on January 6, has almost zero chance of being on the ticket again, according to reports.

Instead, possible names like South Dakota Governor Kristi Noem and South Carolina Senator Tim Scott are being considered.

Noem defended Trump's legacy in the days following the Capitol riots and supported his claims that last year's election was "rigged."

Trump has also publicly endorsed Scott, who is the only black Republican in the Senate, for re-election on Tuesday.

The former president teased the possibility of another bid at the Conservative Political Action Conference (CPAC) this weekend, maintaining his claim that the result of the election was fraudulent, and that he would "beat" the Democrats "for a third time."

Since Trump was acquitted in his impeachment trial last month, he's free to run for office again.

"Donald Trump Will Run Again in 2024, but Will Drop Mike Pence in Favour of Black or Female Running Mate, According to Reports," by Harry Bent, Irish Post March 4, 2021.

Populist conservatism accepts those views but adds something different: the interests and perceptions of "ordinary" people against "elites." So populism rejects the notion of a natural aristocracy of wealth and education, replacing it with the idea that people it considers elites, including career politicians, bureaucrats, journalists and academics, have been promoting their own interests at the expense of regular folk.

The Identity Divide

The recent rise of populism in America has been driven in part by a clear economic reality: The expansion of wealth over the last 40 years has gone almost entirely to the upper reaches of society. At the same time, the middle has stagnated or declined economically.

The populist interpretation is that elites benefited from the globalization and technological advancements they encouraged, while the advantages of those trends bypassed ordinary working people. Calls for trade protections and national borders appeal to Americans who feel left behind.

Populism also has a cultural aspect: rejection of the perceived condescension and smugness of the "highly educated elite."

In that sense, populism is driven by identity (who someone believes they are like, and perhaps more importantly, who they are not like). For populists, the like-minded are ordinary folk—middle income, middle-brow educations at public high schools and state universities, often middle-of-the-country—and the dissimilar are the products of expensive educations and urban lifestyles.

While traditional conservatism has not vanished from the GOP, populist perceptions dominate the new working-class foundations of the party. And those reflect the emerging divide in education.

The base of the Republican Party has shifted from more wealthy and educated Americans to voters without college degrees. In the 1990s, whites who did not attend college tended to back Democrat Bill Clinton, but in 2016 they supported Republican Trump over Democrat Hillary Clinton by 39 percentage points. In 2020, it was roughly the same for Trump over Biden.

The 2020 Outcome and the GOP Future

We believe the Republican Party will be slow to move away from this new identity.

Even after a pandemic, a recession, an impeachment, four years of anti-immigration sentiment and the Black Lives Matter protests, Trump still received more votes than any presidential candidate in history not named Joe Biden.

Biden's overall victory was by a margin of 7 million votes. But his victory in the Electoral College relied on a total of 45,000 votes in three states. This was similar to Trump's narrow 2016 Electoral College margin of 77,000 votes, also in three states. A strong Republican candidate, a foreign policy problem for the incumbent Democrat or a small piece of luck could shift the presidency back to the other party.

Support for Republicans even grew somewhat among traditionally Democratic African American and Hispanic voters, despite the GOP's anti-Black Lives Matter and anti-immigrant rhetoric.

Clearly, Trumpism was not repudiated by voters in the way that Democrats had hoped. It is entirely possible that if the pandemic had not occurred—which was a major source of the decline in his support—Donald Trump would still be in the White House.

The GOP could conclude that its loss was only due to an outside event and not a fundamental rejection of policy. That would give the party little incentive to change course, aside from changing the face on the poster.

Over the next four years we believe the GOP will solidify the transition to a populist base, though not without resistance from traditional conservatives.

Republican victory in a future presidential election would likely require an alliance between traditional and populist conservatives, with both groups turning out to vote. The question is which one will lead the coalition.

The competition for the 2024 Republican nomination will likely also be a contest between these two party bases and ideologies, with the emerging winner defining the post-Trump GOP.

The 2024 Standard Bearers

The Republican contenders for the 2024 nomination and the new leadership of the GOP include a broad range of populists versus traditional conservatives.

Perhaps a leading indicator of the move toward polished populism is the shift in the rhetoric employed by Marco Rubio.

The senator from Florida was once a traditional conservative, but has shifted toward populism after his trouncing by Trump in the 2016 Republican presidential primary. Recently he argued that "the future of the party is based on a multiethnic, multiracial, working-class coalition," defined as "normal, everyday people who don't want to live in a city where there is no police department, where people rampage through the streets every time they are upset about something."

The opposing trend toward rejecting Trumpist populism is exemplified by the shift in the arguments made by Nikki Haley. Haley, the U.N. ambassador under the Trump administration and former South Carolina governor, has rejected Trump's leadership, now arguing that "we shouldn't have followed him."

These two Republicans and several others see a potential president in the mirror. Which one mirrors the current GOP will depend on the realignment or retrenchment between the populists and the traditionalists.

Polished populism—Trump's policies without his personality— may be the future of the GOP's identity.

> *"Trumpism is a reaction to the rather stupendous failure of our elites these last 50 or 60 years. They have given us unwinnable wars and sent our best kids abroad to die in them. They also sent our best jobs—making things—abroad."*

Trump Squandered His Movement

Pittsburgh Post-Gazette *Editorial Board*

In the following viewpoint, the editorial board of the Pittsburgh Post-Gazette *newspaper reexamines Donald Trump's presidency, finding some good ideas about trade and the culture wars but expressing repulsion at the man himself and his actions—from separating children from their parents at the southern border to holding aloft a Bible to signal his supposed piety. The editors deem "woke" culture to be almost as oppressive as Trump himself and believe that many Americans, faced with increasing criticism for not being politically correct, may flee back to the conservatism of the Republican Party if a more palatable candidate than Trump comes along. The* Pittsburgh Post-Gazette *is western Pennsylvania's largest newspaper.*

As you read, consider the following questions:

1. Which of Trump's policies do the editors favor?
2. What are the four main notions of Trumpism, according to the viewpoint?
3. How did former President Trump change the debate on trade?

In the weeks following the presidential election and preceding his departure from office, Donald Trump managed to do what his enemies, as hard as they tried, could not do in four years: He thoroughly disgraced, discredited and marginalized himself.

By persisting in challenging the election, and then inciting a riot, and thus assaulting American liberal democracy itself, which no president has ever done, Mr. Trump destroyed his own legacy.

Whether that means he is finished politically no one can know. But he has surely sealed his fate with the historians. The last days will overshadow everything else, and the never Trumpers—Republicans who said "I like many of his policies and some of his appointments, but the man is an authoritarian nutcase"—will be vindicated.

But, is it possible to separate Donald Trump from the movement he led, the instincts and impulses he expressed, the yearnings of the people he both inspired and exploited—the "deplorables" and their many silent kin?

The bumper sticker credo of Trumpism can be summarized in four slogan-like notions:

- America first.
- Bring back manufacturing.
- Represent rural and flyover America.
- Disturb, if you cannot dismantle, the elites and their norms of governance and political engagement.

Is there any good in any of that? Anything worth keeping? Or is it all half-baked crankery, or worse?

Again, the historians will have their say on a presidency unlike any other and a social movement populated by people who do not join movements.

But what we can say is that there are some solid instincts in Trumpism, mixed with a fair amount of crankery.

For example, an aggressive trade policy, in which trade is managed and there is reciprocity between trading partners, and American interests and workers are put first, makes great sense. But promising to bring back coal is an empty promise.

Or: Having a secure southern border is simply necessary. But the "wall" was over the top, just as separating children from parents was morally repugnant.

One key flaw in Trumpism is that it is a reaction. It is not a doctrine but a corrective, at best, and a mere posture, at worse.

Trumpism contains no ideal or a worldview from which one can glean a game plan, only those gut precepts.

Still, as a reaction it is a legitimate, even profound, one. Trumpism is a reaction to the rather stupendous failure of our elites these last 50 or 60 years. They have given us unwinnable wars and sent our best kids abroad to die in them. They also sent our best jobs—making things—abroad.

It's a pretty wretched record.

No one asked the people of Lima, Ohio, or Youngstown, or Scranton, Pa., where Joe Biden spent his early years, if they wanted "free trade" and a "global economy." No one asked them about keeping troops in Germany for 80 years after World War II.

Without developing a counter-elite, however—people good at government and thinking about government—the Trumpian reaction was often reduced to the president's tweets and Barnum-like behavior or Huey Long-style rallies, with the traditional remedies of Republican politicians and think tanks as an add-on.

It was the Republican establishment that gave us three originalists on the Supreme Court and the better people who passed through the Trump national security team, many of whom were later fired by the president. The Trump presidency gave us new rhetoric but no new public policy ideas to flesh out the instincts, except on trade.

Mr. Trump did change the debate on trade. Everyone is a managed trader now. When we are out of the storm, and the after-storm, of COVID-19, expect everyone from Mike Pence to Elizabeth Warren to be for managed trade.

Ironically, GOP dogma on trade is now what, for generations, was the position of the labor movement and Roosevelt liberals in the Democratic Party.

In many ways, Mr. Trump blew it. His movement met its moment, but he wore us out before it could take hold.

A Marshall Plan for small-town America, for example, cannot happen any time soon. For we have already spent the money we don't have on COVID-19 bailouts, tax cuts and the border wall.

It is impossible to see how more national debt—we are at $27 trillion-plus—is sustainable.

But the other part of Trumpism that will surely remain predates him and was merely co-opted by him—the conservative pushback in the cultural wars.

As the left continues to press its attacks on free thought and speech, its hostility to traditional values and life choices, its hostility to capitalism, organized religion, history, tradition, the police and the family, more and more Americans are likely to be repulsed.

Cultural conservatism is ever renewed by the coarseness of our culture and the bullying of the political left.

Mr. Trump was the unlikely tribune of cultural conservatism. (He absurdly stood in front of a D.C. church holding up a Bible after a military guard paved his way—never thinking to go into the church and pray.) But that does not mean a better champion will not come along.

A loud "no" to statism and the dominant culture resonates with a great many Americans—roughly 71 million Americans.

If the alternatives are cultural conservatism, or libertarian populism with respect for law, or the smug, controlling PC fascism of the left, many Americans will pick the closest approximation to one of the first two. And that means Republicans and/or Trumpist Republicans. Not feeling the benefits of the supercilious and censorious Twitter mob, many voters will opt for being left alone—with their "guns or religion," and their many other un-woke thoughts.

"All major Western political parties have become increasingly hierarchical and remote from their bases."

Trumpism Cannot Trust the Republican Party

Diana Mary Sitek

In the following viewpoint Diana Mary Sitek writes that disaffected conservatives often turn to charismatic leaders such as Donald Trump, but their movements rarely survive after the leader is no longer a central focus. Republicans should be marching in the streets to support Trump's agenda, Sitek states, but nothing of the sort has happened, as renegade Republicans attack Trump with the ferocity of liberals. These Republicans wish only to preserve the status quo. Conservative America, Sitek believes, must organize its own grassroots campaigns to promote the agenda that Trump so ably set in motion. Diana Mary Sitek is a writer who has contributed articles to American Thinker.

As you read, consider the following questions:

1. How does the author feel about Trump's presidency?
2. What is the author's opinion on "woke" culture?
3. What is the viewpoint's recommendation for combatting the liberal elite?

"Can Trumpism Survive?" by Diana Mary Sitek, American Thinker, July 11, 2020. Reprinted by permission.

We know why Trump won the 2016 election. Apart from Hillary Rodham Clinton's frivolous itinerary for snowflakes, the Republican elite had willfully ignored offshore manufacturing's corrosive desolation of local communities and underrated the ricochet effect of Obama's radicalism. Can this political critique by Trump's forsaken middle of the nation build a new conservative narrative, or will Trumpism be a mere four-year flash in the pan? The viability of the Republic may be at stake.

According to political scientist Piero Ignazi, abandoned conservatives typically depend on a single charismatic leader, emerging beyond the party structure. This leader attracts support through outspoken populist language (in Trump's case, his tweets). Mobilization via mass rallies rather than grassroots participation is its defining characteristic. Ignazi warns that seldom does the movement survive the leader's exit from the political arena. The party exploits the charismatic leader it often disdains to retain power for itself.

Recently, I received a request for money from the local Republican branch. Instead of writing a check, I politely inquired why the people in charge had not organized street marches promoting Trump's agenda. Where are the Republican-sponsored demonstrations for "Freedom of Speech and Peaceful Streets," for "All Lives Matter" and "Restore the Constitution," for "Drain the Swamp," "Cancel the Propaganda Curriculum," and "Prosecute the Slanderous Media"? Not a peep in response.

Even more alarming than the party's tepid support for the president is the disloyalty of disaffected NeverTrumps. They are grievously offended and have barricaded themselves in the Lincoln Project, which is currently airing television advertisements hostile to the president. Their aim—"to defeat Donald Trump and Trumpism." Following the lines of the left's demolition schedule, they plan to bulldoze Congress and the Senate (in order to save them), sparing only the RINOs. Democrats, the MSM, and fatuous retired generals are applauding.

THE FUTURE IS TRUMPISM

Staking his claim to the Republican Party, former President Donald Trump is casting his populist policies and attack-dog politics as the key to future GOP success.

In a closed-door speech Saturday night to donors at his Mar-a-Lago resort, Trump also reinforced his commitment to the party, according to prepared remarks obtained by the Associated Press. His appearance came as Republican officials are trying to play down an internal feud over Trump's role in the party, his commitment to GOP fundraising and his plans for 2024. While Trump's advisers reported he would emphasize party unity, he did not, according to reported accounts of attendees, stick to the script.

He called Senate Republican leader Mitch McConnell—who drew particular ire from the Trump camp for frank remarks on Trump's responsibility for the Jan. 6 siege on the US Capitol following the former president's second impeachment acquittal—a "dumb son of a b----," according to insider accounts.

Trump also reportedly repeated his contention that it was a lack of courage rather than the Constitution and fact that prevented then–Vice President Mike Pence from blocking the congressional certification of President Joe Biden's electoral victory on Jan. 6.

"The key to this triumphant future will be to build on the gains our amazing movement has made over the past four years," Trump, in his scripted remarks, told hundreds of leading Republican donors, according to the prepared remarks. "Under our leadership, we welcomed millions upon millions of new voters into the Republican coalition. We transformed the Republican Party into a party that truly fights for all Americans."

It was the final address of the Republican National Committee's weekend donor summit in Palm Beach. Most of the RNC's invitation-only gathering was held at a luxury hotel a few miles away; attendees were bused to Trump's club for his remarks.

While a significant faction of the Republican Party hopes to move past Trump's divisive leadership, the location of the event suggests that the GOP, at least for now, considers Trump its undisputed leader and chief fundraiser.

"Trump Says the Future of the Republican Party Is Trumpism," Marketwatch, April 12, 2021.

Consequently, Trumpism cannot trust the Republican Party. However, all major Western political parties have become increasingly hierarchical and remote from their bases. They are indistinguishable from the State's expanding apparatus of power. They nominate its mandarins and pander to its clients (for a price), snubbing the sheep below.

A powerful corrective to this malaise of being passed over by political elites sprang up in the mushrooming of radical grassroots activist movements on the left, from feminist to green to Antifa to BLM. Grassroots organizing surmounts that frustrated desire for direct political participation. It provides a renewed sense of identity amid the chaos of tumbling institutions—the very institutions the grassroots activists have been directed to pull down by the post-truth "wokeness" of university professors!

Thus, the politicized NGO is both weapon and remedy. Its most outstanding success was the 9/11 attack. The Twin Towers were not only office space, but monumental statues memorializing American capitalism. Organized Islamic cadres have furnished a state-of-the-art revolutionary model for insurrectionists to emulate, from toppling statues to proclaiming independent no-go zones to Ilhan Omar's call for the "dismantling" of entire economic and political systems.

The Democrat Party is now hostage to these deranged malcontents for its very survival. It cannot move to the center. Globalists, such as George Soros and GAFA (Google, Apple, Facebook, Amazon), have taken full advantage of this phenomenon. They have gilded anti-conservative NGOs to the hilt, handing over to them supervision of permissible speech, the purgation of civil institutions, and more recently swarming the streets with staged revolutionary pantomime and homicidal live theatrical events.

Why are there so few political mass organizations on the right? Because moderate conservatives are guardians of historical heritage. They wish to preserve the Republic's longstanding institutions and assumed they were already protected. Wrong! The left is hell-bent on razing them to the ground. The Hill advises, correctly, that "[the] conservative challenge is to activate [its] citizens. As the Left proved ... this requires more than just television ads or digital campaigns. Grassroots infrastructure is the crucial factor. This, more than anything, is where conservatives need to invest."

During Obama's presidency, we saw the beginning of a viable grassroots conservative political movement in the Tea Party. By weaponizing the IRS, Obama butchered that nascent movement (for which unconstitutional act he suffered no legal pain). We cannot allow this to recur.

Heritage Action (affiliated with the conservative Heritage Foundation) is an exemplar of how to rescue Trump's conservatism from annihilation. It combines inside-the-Beltway lobbying with outside-the-Beltway grassroots pressure through its Sentinel program. Check it out. There are others. Find one and participate!

Under brutal daily attack, Trump has championed an existential defense against the left's heinous program of "tearing down the system." Bravely, he has sown a fresh field of conservative seeds, but he cannot singlehandedly guarantee the crop. The left has militarized its grassroots. Therefore, without a regiment of militant, conservative NGOs, we lack the necessary weapons to fight those who wish to despoil our crops and turn our Republic into a weed-choked wasteland. Remaining for any longer "the silent majority" raises a white flag and loudly proclaims our surrender.

> "The campaign promises Trump
> originally ran on are still appealing
> and would likely be more successful
> without Trump himself heading
> their implementation."

Trumpism Is Better Off Without Trump

Jonathan Kyncl

In the following viewpoint Jonathan Kyncl describes a talk given by conservative gadfly Ann Coulter at a Turning Point USA event. While Coulter originally supported Trump and still supports his agenda, she has turned away from the former president, in part because of his inability to implement his policies. She believes that going forward, Trumpism is better off without its eponymous leader. While Coulter expressed disappointment with Republicans' inability to enact their agenda, she believed that they were on the correct path, opining that there are many bad Republicans but no good Democrats. Jonathan Kyncl is a reporter for OUDaily, the independent student voice of the University of Oklahoma.

"'Going on with Trumpism Without Trump,' Ann Coulter Speaks at OU Turning Point USA Student Event," by Jonathan Kyncl, OuDaily, November 5, 2020. Reprinted by permission.

As you read, consider the following questions:

1. Where does Ann Coulter see similarities between Trump's agenda and that of Bernie Sanders?
2. How does Coulter often use hyperbole in her messaging?
3. Why were there protests outside of the venue where Coulter spoke?

At a university in the heart of a historically red state, Republican political pundit Ann Coulter expressed disdain for President Donald Trump while a majority of the crowd nodded in agreement.

Coulter, a featured speaker at the Turning Point USA event, continued while protests began in front of the Oklahoma Memorial Union against the event.

Though Coulter has repeatedly expressed distaste for the incumbent president both on Twitter and in podcasts, she said the campaign promises Trump originally ran on are still appealing and would likely be more successful without Trump himself heading their implementation.

"The Trump agenda without Trump would be a lot easier," Coulter said. "Our new motto should be 'Going on with Trumpism without Trump.' That's a winning strategy."

Though she questioned Trump's ability to implement many of his policies, Coulter said the Republican Party would be well-served to keep the current president as "the rally guy," whether he secures another term or is defeated by former Vice President Joe Biden in the ongoing election.

Coulter said that Trump and Vermont Sen. Bernie Sanders had similar views with populist issues, adding that the political left and right should be able to unite to address issues like immigration and job creation.

"The populist issues are issues that Donald Trump and Bernie Sanders' positions were really close on, at least for some of the things I care about," Coulter said. "The Democrat Party is socialist. (Voters are) being scammed on the populist issues that (they) ought to come together on, left and right, to get together in politics. It's a class issue, and I don't want to burn down the rich, but I do think there could be a little more fairness for our fellow Americans."

Coulter voiced that Trump has suffered historic attacks by the media, but these attacks have made his presidency look more impressive.

"The only people in the world who think saying something is the same as doing something are the media and Trump. The media acted like whatever Trump said just miraculously happened ... so attacking him for the things he said, not the things he did, made him look great," Coulter said. "Trump faced historic resistance from the media, and still about half of the people said, 'I'm not voting for (Democrats), I'm not voting for the media.'"

Coulter also spoke on many issues concerning conservative beliefs, including the Supreme Court possibly overturning *Roe v. Wade*.

"I don't think *Roe v. Wade* will be overturned until we have at least a solid majority, as the one that put it into law," Coulter said. "(Overturning Roe v. Wade) doesn't mean abortion is unconstitutional, doesn't make it illegal. All it does is say there's not a constitutional right and (it) should be decided the way everything else is inside the department ... I promise you, California, really the whole West coast, you will be able to abort a child until they turn 30."

Coulter also stated that another main issue in the US currently is voter fraud within the election.

"Trump wins Michigan, 'Oh, we still need to count Detroit.' Trump wins Georgia, 'Oh, we still need to count Atlanta.'... this is how voter fraud happens," Coulter said. "So every time Democrats scream bloody murder, but when Republicans want to investigate voter fraud, then (Democrats) say it doesn't happen, but that's because they wont investigate it ... By that theory there were no lynchings of Black men in the South because we don't have any convictions."

Despite the indecisive state of the presidential election at the time of Coulter's speech, she celebrated the Republican Party's performance in the national Congressional elections, particularly the party earning new seats in the House of Representatives and fighting to defend their majority hold on the Senate.

Approximately 25 protesters outside of the event were expressing their anger for Coulter coming to speak at OU.

Biology junior Logan Pesina, the Students Advocates Against Government Injustice COVID-19 officer, said this event inviting Coulter "doesn't align with beliefs including diversion and inclusion" at the university. Pesina expressed that Coulter's presence does not make her feel safe, adding that TPUSA's "paying for her to be here is terrifying."

These protesters were also met with roughly 25 counter-protesters, including men wearing "Proud Boys" attire, who were there to advocate for Coulter. The two groups of protesters were heard tossing jeers toward each other, including "fascist" and "racist."

While the protests continued, Coulter ended the event by taking questions from the eager audience, including those addressing the "Democratic hunt for racism."

"With Joe Biden, it's going to be racism all the time. Racism is truly a bad thing but unless it's acted upon, it's not in the top 100 of worst things," Coulter said. "Upon graduating, every college should tell their students, 'Go into the real world so you can find racism.' Finding racism doesn't produce anything … any time or money being spent on finding racism won't help anything."

Coulter stated that many college graduates are "useless" because they have numerous student loans and majors that will not get them a job to make money. Coulter said colleges should back their own student loans based on a major's projected average salary to combat federal student loan debt.

"People are wasting money doing this gender studies and ethnic studies, and they can never pay back their student loans, just to get a job in a Starbucks after graduation," Coulter said. "I don't know the future of engineering with STEM fields once we stop letting in low-wage immigrants here to take those jobs, and there are such jobs out of college. Colleges need to just stop supporting all these massive, richer jobs that graduates (can) do."

Coulter also voiced that Democrats' failure to support a border wall translated to the party's desire for "hundreds of millions of poor people" to enter the country.

Near the end of the event, Coulter summarized her feelings towards the Democratic party in a short statement.

"There are a lot of bad Republicans, there are no good Democrats," Coulter said.

> "The political logic of Trumpism resided in ideological and electoral opportunities—namely, solidifying the GOP among its new more-Evangelical voters, and reaching out over and over again to the remnants of Reagan Democrats and other groups that have been globalization's losers."

Trumpism Will Prevail

Michael Brendan Dougherty

While many observers believe that Trumpism cannot survive without Trump, in the following viewpoint, Michael Brendan Dougherty disagrees. Trumpism is a movement, a populist-national response to the missteps of the global-oriented United States government. Even if the movement is occasionally annoying, it is still headed in the right direction—away from foreign entanglements and toward an America first agenda. While Trump may no longer be in the national picture, his voters remain a powerful force in American politics. Michael Brendan Dougherty is a senior writer at National Review *and a national correspondent for the* American Conservative.

"Trumpism After Trump," by Michael Brendan Dougherty, National Review, January 18, 2021. Reprinted by permission.

As you read, consider the following questions:

1. How does the viewpoint's first paragraph get the reader's attention?
2. How does the global picture reinforce the notion that Trumpism is not going away?
3. How, according to the author, does America's foreign relations with China demand a Trumpist response?

Will Trumpism survive President Donald Trump? For many observers, the answer is obvious: no. Trumpism is about Donald Trump, and only Donald Trump, and it has no substance beyond that. It is a rhetoric and an affect, in service to him, and that's on its best days. On most others, it is a gibbering cult and series of baroque conspiracy theories. Trumpism is just a giant sucking sound around the black hole of the man's own vanity. It will eventually disappear, as he has, up his own backside.

This is, I think, incorrect. Trumpism is a populist-nationalist politics. It is populist because it preaches political doctrines largely rejected by the incumbent political class: an America-first foreign policy, revision of the aims of our trade policy, and a halt to mass migration. It is a nationalist project whose ultimate aim is to restore the democratic link between the citizenry and government—a link that has been threatened by a class of "experts" who govern a subordinate native class on behalf of oligarchic interests. Trumpism seeks a political mandate from the losers of post–Cold War globalization. It chafes at the restraints of a "world order" when it does not suit the national interest. It is the restorationist character of this nationalist project that makes it appealing to many conservatives and, ultimately, an ally of conservatism—even if an occasionally annoying or obstreperous one.

Five years ago, I predicted that Trump would probably damage—perhaps irretrievably—the populist and nationalist causes he championed in the GOP. And he has roughly followed the script I laid out. His inconstancy and self-interest have often led to him to betray or leave incomplete the populist and nationalist policies he championed. We haven't moved to the skills-based immigration system he promised. We haven't fully withdrawn from long wars where there is no reasonable hope of a satisfying conclusion or national objective to be achieved. Trump's trade war with China concluded without any fundamental changes to the economic and political dynamics of the Sino-American relationship.

And in recent weeks, his behavior has brought further disrepute to these causes. He made his claims of material electoral fraud a dividing line for his party. This GOP then lost the votes of the Georgia Republicans who believed that the presidential election had been stolen and that the state party was ignoring their concerns—which led to the GOP's losing control of the Senate. Feeding his hardest-core supporters with the conspiracy theory led some of them to storm the US Capitol in riotous violence, leaving five dead. Those who opposed him chiefly to resist populist and nationalist accretions to conservative politics have been given the weapons to potentially exclude him from discussions about the future of the Republican Party. Trump's failures as a president, and the political failures of the GOP under him, will be used against populist-nationalism, by its critics on the right and left. They will be used opportunistically, just as the failings of Bush have been used against neoconservatives who eventually embraced him.

And yet, it's not over.

To understand whether Trumpism has a future in the Republican Party, it's important to consider "Trumpism before Trump." It has been tempting to view Trumpism as a minor and electorally inert heresy. It has never had any real champions in the Senate. The giant phalanx of conservative institutions—think tanks, party leaders, and media outlets—were against Trumpism. It is, the critics say, just Pat Buchananism and revived only because Donald Trump was a celebrity and an innovative campaigner.

This is not true. While Trump's celebrity is an underrated factor in his success, looking backward from 2021, Trumpism seems inevitable and on the rise, with many antecedent figures across the party championing at least parts of it. Ronald Reagan used tariffs to defend American icon Harley-Davidson. Patrick Buchanan and his allied paleo-conservatives denounced the first Iraq War and attacked George H. W. Bush on the cultural issues, particularly the Civil Rights Act of 1991.

Before the ideological transformation in the wake of 9/11, George W. Bush ran in 2000 on a more constrained foreign policy. He preached "the modesty of true strength" and "the humility of real greatness." And his national-security adviser, Condoleezza Rice, tilted against an American foreign policy that aimed at "second order" effects, such as the advancement of human rights. He also used tariffs in an attempt to hold Ohio and add Pennsylvania to the Republican coalition.

Arguably the last two contenders in the 2012 Republican primary were Trumpists of a sort. Rick Santorum was critical of free trade. Mitt Romney showed something of a Trumpist ability to get to Rick Perry's right on immigration, while being more supportive of the welfare state. If Romney had been elected, we might now have a more Trumpist trade arrangement with China than even Trump has sought.

The political logic of Trumpism resided in ideological and electoral opportunities—namely, solidifying the GOP among its new more-Evangelical voters, and reaching out over and over again to the remnants of Reagan Democrats and other groups that have been globalization's losers—voters who have been effectively abandoned by a Democratic Party dominated by college-educated lifestyle progressives.

In fact, one big clue that "Trumpism" won't just go away with Trump is that the phenomenon is global. Many left-leaning parties across the world made their peace with global capitalism after 1989, abandoning their traditional workers in favor of culturally progressive, upwardly mobile, educated voters; they centered themselves instead on the new professionals in global cities. That shift has inevitably generated failures and resentments, left and right. On the left, it inspired Syriza in Greece and a short vogue for old-school nationally focused socialists like Bernie Sanders in the US, Jeremy Corbyn in the U.K., and Jean-Luc Mélenchon in France. It also inspired a broader movement on the right. The rise of Trumpism in the US, Brexit in Britain including Johnson's smash-through in Labour heartlands, and the advent of Lega under Matteo Salvini in Italy are all connected by dissatisfaction with a politics of the 1990s.

And there are reasons to believe that political conditions will continue to call for a Trumpist response for some time.

The most obvious reason for this is China. Free trade has often been accepted by conservatives as simply efficient. But in the case of China, it has been defended by citing larger theories about the world that have proven untrue—namely, that trade liberalization would lead to political liberalization in China and that any losses owing to America's strategy of low-wage labor arbitrage would be diffuse and easily ameliorated through redistribution of the gains. None of this has proved true, and what is called "free trade" by Americans is clearly seen by the Chinese as mercantile and industrial policy for China's geostrategic benefit.

In the way that America's Silicon Valley behemoths tended to transmit American ideas of free speech worldwide (at least at first), Chinese commercial firms are now proving to be extensions of the Chinese Communist Party, dedicated to total political control. As China's economy grows larger than America's, the rate at which CCP values are transmitted across the world will increase. Inasmuch as "globalization" means Sinicization, Americans are likely to resist it.

While the great mass movements of migration from 2015 have slowed down, the truth is that technological advancements have dramatically lowered the financial and psychological price of emigration from the third world to the first. Borders are hardening all over the world in response to this reality, and they are likely to do so here as well.

Finally, the truth is that those "left-behind" voters of the old left-wing coalitions as well as many other voters have been deprived of institutions. They exist in smaller, more fragmented networks. They are less likely to be a part of labor unions or members of churches. They are therefore less likely to be the kind of traditional small-c conservatives who hope to preserve their little platoons and who are content and therefore fearful of change. Instead, they are more likely to be dissatisfied with many present arrangements, and they are open to the broad appeal of politics in a nationalist key, which promises solidarity based on shared membership in the nation, and which seeks to reorder the priorities of the governing class to bring them in line with their own aims and well-being. Working with these voters presents serious challenges and even dangers for traditional conservatives. We've seen many of those dangers these last five years. But there are many more opportunities as well.

Trump may be leaving the national stage, but the voters he brought into the coalition and the challenges he identified are not going anywhere.

> "A prerequisite for getting off our
> current path is to understand that we
> chose to get on it in the first place. So
> much of what ails us is self-inflicted.
> We feel ourselves to be in the grip of
> macro-forces beyond our control, but
> they derive their power from millions
> of micro-choices we made."

Centrism Is the Cure for a Divided Nation

Katherine C. Epstein

*In the following excerpted viewpoint Katherine C. Epstein observes
that meeting in the center is the only way to combat the extreme
division that currently characterizes US politics. Sticking to bedrock
principles and not being swayed by short term gains is a must if our
current political system is to survive. Epstein suggests that liberals
and conservatives have much more in common than they will admit,
and that America's current political wounds are self-inflicted. Only by
stressing our commonalities and not our differences will the country
start on the road to healing. Katherine C. Epstein is associate professor
of history at Rutgers University-Camden and author of* Torpedo:
Inventing the Military-Industrial Complex in the United States
and Great Britain.

"The Tolling Bell," by Katherine C. Epstein, American Purpose, March 26, 2021. Reprinted
by permission.

As you read, consider the following questions:

1. According to the viewpoint, how did Martin Luther King Jr. sacrifice short-term gains for long-term improvements?
2. According to Epstein, who is a Democrat, what does she have in common with Trump voters?
3. What type of leaders are needed to help end the extreme divisions of our times?

[...]

Mutual dehumanization is the path to human desolation on a scale that goes well beyond the unhappiness of our current moment. Democracies cannot survive when neither side is prepared to lose, and when the perception of an emergency makes both sides willing to sacrifice their principles but unwilling to compromise. Professed emergencies have a way of becoming real ones. Democrats and Republicans are fools if they think their parties can win or survive in a real emergency. Political violence destroys institutions, or it allows them to survive only in a morally debased form.

The only way to get off the path we're on is centrism. This is a dirty word in American politics—and for political machines, a scary one. Tellingly, both sides speak with contempt for centrists, as though marauding bands of moderates are what threaten the American experiment.

It's true that there is a negative form of centrism, defined by relative distance from the poles, that offers no succor. There's also a form of moderation, like that lacerated by King, which is really moral cowardice. But I'm talking about a positive centrism, defined by commitment to bedrock principles of liberal democracy, even and especially when they don't immediately produce the outcome we want. The bedrock principles of liberal democracy happen to be the same as the bedrock principles of humanistic scholarship, which are process-oriented rather than outcome-oriented.

By this definition of centrism, King, who defended extremism for love, was a moderate for sticking to his nonviolent principles, even though they promised only suffering in the short term. He not only sought to hold a center between opposing forces in the African-American community; he also identified and held the vital center of the whole American nation. This vital center can accommodate widely divergent policy preferences; King himself (contra his admirers on the right and critics on the left) had a radical political-economic vision. The key is that everyone agrees to play by the procedural ground rules of liberal democracy.

A prerequisite for getting off our current path is to understand that we chose to get on it in the first place. So much of what ails us is self-inflicted. We feel ourselves to be in the grip of macro-forces beyond our control, but they derive their power from millions of micro-choices we made. Jack Dorsey didn't personally hold a gun to the head of everyone who signed up for Twitter, and Citizens United didn't make you forward that glib political meme. Godless socialists don't force conservatives to say "cry more, lib," and neoliberalism didn't force Elizabeth Warren to tell her "joke." The dopamine hit that comes from the thrill of group viciousness is just more appealing than the hard work of trying to understand each other in all our complexity. The consequences ultimately result from our own human frailty.

I often suspect that I have much in common with many Trump voters. Most people, including me, just want a quiet life, I think. We are content to live and die, in Thomas Gray's exquisite words, either "some mute inglorious Milton" or "some Cromwell guiltless of his country's blood." Of course people have different ideas about what constitutes a quiet life, and those differences can produce great disquiet, especially when those who seek an unquiet life exploit them. Moreover, the desire for quietude tips all too easily into the acquiescence of King's white moderate.

But it's a vanishingly small number of human beings who wake up in the morning and go, "How can I be evil today?" (perhaps as few as those who wake up and ask themselves how they can serve the greater good). Most of us are just trying to survive, ideally with at least some ability to think well of ourselves. The human need to see our choices as good, even when what they really are is easy, drives our enormous capacity for rationalization, as well as our less enormous capacity to stop rationalizing.

I have no doubt that many Trump voters cast their votes on the mirror image of the rationalization that impels mine. I vote for the Democratic Party not because it attracts me but because the Republican Party repels me marginally more. My votes in 2016 and 2020 were not for Clinton or for Biden but against Trump. Trump simply could not have won election without people who are my political inverse, those who voted against Clinton rather than for Trump. He had to win the votes of people who are, say, 55/45 Republican, just as Clinton won my vote because I'm 55/45 Democratic. Ten points separate me from those people; 45 points separate me from those who are 100/0 Democratic. Naturally, the notion of a third party has a distinct allure, though whether it's remotely viable or even desirable are fair questions—a third party, like abolishing the Electoral College, could well have unintended negative consequences. All I know is that when I look at the far Right and the far Left, I think, I don't want to be governed by any of these people.

What I want in leaders is moral and intellectual seriousness. Their positions on discrete issues, even those of great importance to me, have become less of a concern as the realization has dawned that lasting victories on those issues are impossible without a nation to enjoy them in. By all means, our leaders should be interested in the grown-up questions of how and why we got where we are as a nation. But their squabbles over the childish questions of who is most to blame truly could not be less interesting—or more dangerous. They should be able to articulate a vision of America that acknowledges our history of dehumanization, but also our history of humanization; that recognizes the shared Americanness of urban and rural residents, conservatives and liberals, or Republicans and Democrats; and that appeals to the better angels of our nature. They should understand that all Americans are caught in an inescapable network of mutuality, tied in a single garment of national destiny. They should be willing to stand up to their political base when they believe bedrock principles are at stake, and they should be prepared to lovingly accept the consequences. They should treat voters like grown-ups, which means representation when possible but the courtesy of dissent when necessary, rather than pandering. Of course, it would be helpful to have a populace that can tell the difference.

A hallmark of maturity, in both a person and a nation, is the willingness to live with moral complexity. When we build walls among ourselves for fear of moral contamination, should we be surprised that we elect a president whose signature issue is a wall? Our ability to accept moral complexity in others is tied to our ability to accept it in ourselves. An inability to accept it in ourselves is tied to an inability to accept it in others.

The borders between ourselves and others, like the border between human and God created by eating from the Tree of Knowledge, are necessary to have knowledge of ourselves and knowledge of others. That knowledge, like the border that creates it, can be destroyed either by hardening into certainty or by dissolving into nihilism. Its existence is at once the result of original sin and the only hope of redemption. The search for a middle ground between walls and open borders confronts Americans with our most morally and politically urgent task, as it does all humanity.

The bell cannot toll for Trumpism a moment too soon. But it will not until we all hear it tolling for ourselves.

Periodical and Internet Sources Bibliography

The following articles have been selected to supplement the diverse views presented in this chapter.

Associated Press, "Trump says the future of the Republican Party is Trumpism," *Associated Press*, April 12, 2021. https://apnews.com/article/donald-trump-politics-381bf69568bc0bd416e9dbb45aad1af7.

James A. Baker III, "Focus on Principle, Not Personality, for a Bright GOP Future," *Wall Street Journal.* June 6, 2021. https://www.wsj.com/articles/focus-on-principle-not-personality-for-a-bright-gop-future-11623007610.

Alexander Bolton, "GOP wrestles with role of culture wars in party's future," The Hill, May 2, 2021. https://thehill.com/homenews/senate/551331-gop-wrestles-with-role-of-culture-wars-in-partys-future.

Megan DiTrolio and Maria Ricapito, "Grand New Party?" *Marie Claire.* March 5, 2021. https://www.marieclaire.com/politics/a35685385/republican-party-future/.

David Graf, "Q&A with Representative Liz Cheney on the future of the Republican Party," *Wyoming News Now.* May 25, 2021. https://www.wyomingnewsnow.tv/2021/05/26/qa-with-representative-liz-cheney-on-the-future-of-the-republican-party/.

Peter Grier, "The 'big lie,' Liz Cheney, and the future of the Republican Party." *Christian Science Monitor*, May 6, 2021. https://www.csmonitor.com/USA/Politics/2021/0506/The-big-lie-Liz-Cheney-and-the-future-of-the-Republican-Party.

Susan A. Hughes, "What is the future of the Republican party?," Harvard Kennedy School, March 15, 2021. https://www.hks.harvard.edu/faculty-research/policy-topics/politics/what-future-republican-party.

David Jackson, "Paul Ryan says Republicans need to focus on 'principles' and not individuals as Trump remains a force in the party," *USA Today.* May 27, 2021. https://www.usatoday.com/story/news/2021/05/27/donald-trump-and-gop-reagan-group-weighs-republican-party-future/5239025001/.

Mary Louise Kelley, "What Liz Cheney's Removal Means For The Future Of The GOP," NPR. May 12, 2021. https://www.npr.org/2021/05/12/996286582/what-liz-cheney-s-removal-means-for-the-future-of-the-gop.

Ed Kilgore, "The Future Could Actually Be Bright for Republicans." *New York*. May 20, 2021. https://nymag.com/intelligencer/2021/05/the-future-could-actually-be-bright-for-republicans.html.

Rich Lowry, "Lowry: Future is bright for Republican Party," *Boston Herald*. May 22, 2021. https://www.bostonherald.com/2021/05/22/lowry-future-is-bright-for-republican-party/.

Andrew Prokop, "Why the Republican Party can't reckon with Trump," Vox. May 19, 2021. https://www.vox.com/2021/5/19/22440434/trump-mcconnell-commission-january-6.

David Smith, "After Trump, what is the future of the Republican Party?" Conversation. February 18, 2021. https://theconversation.com/after-trump-what-is-the-future-of-the-republican-party-154726.

George F. Will, "Opinion: The Reaganite optimist Paul Ryan on the future of the Republican Party," *Washington Post*. June 9, 2021. https://www.washingtonpost.com/opinions/2021/06/09/reaganite-optimist-paul-ryan-future-republican-party/.

For Further Discussion

Chapter 1

1. After reading the viewpoints in this chapter, how would you define Trumpism?
2. How would you distinguish between Trumpism and political conservatism?
3. Does Trumpism seem to be a viable political philosophy going forward or must it be modified in order to succeed on a national level?

Chapter 2

1. Was President Trump successful, unsuccessful, or some combination of the two during his four years in office? Use information from the viewpoints in this chapter to make your case.
2. After reading conflicting articles on Space Force, do you think this new branch of the military is an important step forward or an unnecessary indulgence?
3. Do you think the concept of America First advances US policy domestically and abroad? Why or why not?

Chapter 3

1. Has Donald Trump legitimately threatened democracy in America, or is this an overblown notion advanced by liberals?
2. In what specific ways do the viewpoints in this chapter argue that Trump threatened democracy in the United States?
3. Does the Capitol riot of January 6, 2021, along with other political violence, pose a legitimate threat to democracy? Why or why not?

Chapter 4

1. After reading the viewpoints in this chapter, what is your opinion concerning the future of the Republican party?
2. Is Trump still the primary force in Republican politics moving forward? Why or why not?
3. Based on this chapter's viewpoints, how might the so-called Republican "civil war" resolve itself?

Organizations to Contact

The editors have compiled the following list of organizations concerned with the issues debated in this book. The descriptions are derived from materials provided by the organizations. All have publications or information available for interested readers. The list was compiled on the date of publication of the present volume; the information provided here may change. Be aware that many organizations take several weeks or longer to respond to inquiries, so allow as much time as possible.

American Civil Liberties Union (ACLU)

125 Broad Street New York NY 10004-2400
(212) 549-2500
website: www.aclu.org

The ACLU considers itself to be the nation's guardian of liberty, working in courts, legislatures, and communities to defend and preserve the individual rights and liberties that the Constitution and the laws of the United States guarantee. Among the issues they focus on are human rights, racial equality, and women's rights. Among their key interests are voting rights and religious liberty.

American Enterprise Institute for Public Policy Research (AEI)

American Enterprise Institute
1789 Massachusetts Avenue NW
Washington, DC 20036
(202)862-5800
email: tyler.castle@aei.org
website: www.aei.org

The American Enterprise Institute is a conservative public policy think tank that sponsors original research on the world economy, US foreign policy and international security, and domestic political and social issues. AEI is dedicated to defending human dignity, expanding human potential, and building a freer and safer world. Their scholars and staff advance ideas rooted in their belief in democracy and free enterprise. AEI's website has reports on topics such as democracy's health and collaboration in Congress. One of their projects is the Survey Center on American Life, which features a number of insightful surveys and articles on the Trump presidency.

The Bipartisan Policy Center

1225 Eye Street NW, Suite 1000
Washington, DC 20005
(202) 204 - 2400
email: bipartisaninfo@bipartisanpolicy.org
website: www.bipartisanpolicy.org

The Bipartisan Policy Center is a Washington, DC-based think tank that actively fosters bipartisanship by combining the best ideas from both parties to promote health, security, and opportunity for all Americans. Their policy solutions are the product of informed deliberations by former elected and appointed officials, business and labor leaders, and academics and advocates who represent both sides of the political spectrum. According to its website, BPC prioritizes one thing above all else: getting things done.

Brookings Institute

The Brookings Institution
1775 Massachusetts Avenue NW
Washington, DC 20036
(202) 797-6000
email: communications@brookings.edu
website: www.brookings.edu

The Brookings Institution is a nonprofit public policy organization based in Washington, DC. Their mission is to conduct in-depth research that leads to new ideas for solving problems facing society at the local, national, and global level. Brookings brings together more than three hundred leading experts in government and academia from all over the world who provide research, policy recommendations, and analysis on a full range of public policy issues. Their research agenda and recommendations are rooted in open-minded inquiry and represent diverse points of view. Research topics cover foreign policy, economics, development, governance, and metropolitan policy. Their website features podcasts such as "Defending truth from the war on facts," and articles such as: "Where Midwesterners struggle, Trumpism lives on," and "Will Trumpism change Republican foreign policy permanently?"

Cato Institute

1000 Massachusetts Avenue NW
Washington, DC 20001-5403
(202) 842-0200
web site: www.cato.org

The Cato Institute is a libertarian public policy research organization, a think tank dedicated to the principles of individual liberty, limited government, free markets, and peace. Its scholars and analysts conduct independent research on a wide range of policy issues. Articles on their website include "Is 'Trumpism without Trump' the GOP's Future?" They also feature several podcasts concerning Trumpism.

Center for American Progress (*CAP*)

1333 H Street NW, 10th Floor
Washington, DC 20005
(202) 682-1611
website: www.americanprogress.org

The Center for American Progress is a public policy research and advocacy organization which presents a liberal viewpoint on economic and social issues. Their website contains reports on topics such as democracy and government; and politics and elections.

Freedom House

1850 M Street NW, 11th Floor
Washington DC 20036
(202) 296-5101.
email: info@freedomhouse.org
Website: http://freedomhouse.org

Freedom House advocates for a US foreign policy that places the promotion of democracy as a priority. Its representatives regularly testify before Congress, provide briefings to high level administration and US State Department officials, and argue the case for freedom at conferences, in op-eds, and through media appearances. Freedom House serves as a leading advocate for policies to advance worldwide democracy. Its website contains numerous relevant materials, including a section on "Election Integrity."

The Heritage Foundation

214 Massachusetts Avenue NE
Washington, DC 20002-4999
(800) 546-2843
email: info@heritage.org
website: www.heritage.org

The Heritage Foundation is a conservative think tank. The organization's mission is to formulate and promote conservative public policies based on the principles of free enterprise, limited government, individual freedom, traditional American values, and a strong national defense. Their searchable website considers issues such as election integrity, the Constitution, and immigration.

Mises Institute

518 West Magnolia Avenue
Auburn, AL 36832-4501
(334) 321-2100
website: www.mises.org

Mises Institute is a Libertarian think tank in researching and promoting viewpoints about subjects such as economics, philosophy, and political economy. Named for the famous Austrian School economist, the institute's stated mission is to promote "the Misesian tradition of thought through the defense of the market economy, private property, sound money, and peaceful international relations, while opposing government intervention." While many have labeled them a conservative organization, they resist that notion, arguing that their foreign policy views, their position on the US Constitution, and their views on social policy are all either nonconservative or anti-conservative. Their website features articles such as "Why Trumpism Might Bring a New Era for Political Parties" and "The Future of Trump's Populism," that are also available in audio format.

National Endowment for Democracy (NED)

1025 F Street NW, Suite 800
Washington, DC 20004
(202) 378-9700
email: info@NED.org
website: www.ned.org

Founded in 1983, the National Endowment for Democracy (NED) is a private, nonprofit foundation dedicated to the growth and strengthening of democratic institutions around the world. NED is dedicated to fostering the growth of a wide range of democratic institutions abroad, including political parties, trade unions, free markets, and business organizations, as well as the many elements of a vibrant civil society that ensure human rights, an independent media, and the rule of law.

Bibliography of Books

Tim Alberta. *American Carnage: On the Front Lines of the Republican Civil War and the Rise of President Trump*. New York, NY: Harper, 2020.

Noah Berlatsky. *The Republican Party: [opposing Viewpoints]*. Farmington Hills, MI: Greenhaven Press, 2015.

John R. Bolton. *The Room Where It Happened: A White House Memoir*. New York, NY: Encounter Books, 2020.

Barbara Brodman and James E. Doan. *Utopia and Dystopia in the Age of Trump: Images from Literature and Visual Arts*. Madison, New Jersey: Fairleigh Dickinson University Press; Lanham, MD: Rowman & Littlefield, 2019.

Amanda B. Carpenter. *Gaslighting America: Why We Love It When Trump Lies to Us*. New York, NY: Broadside Books, 2018.

Chris Christie. *Let Me Finish: Trump, the Kushners, Bannon, New Jersey, and the Power of In-Your-Face Politics*. New York, NY: Hachette, 2019.

William Connolly. *Aspirational Fascism: The Struggle for Multifaceted Democracy UnderTrumpism*. Minneapolis, MN: University of Minnesota Press, 2017.

E. J. Dionne, *Why the Right Went Wrong: Conservatism —from Goldwater to the Tea Party and Beyond*. New York, NY: Simon and Schuster, 2016

David Frum. *Trumpocracy: The Corruption of the American Republic*. New York, NY: HarperCollins, 2018.

Ben Fountain. *Beautiful Country Burn Again: Democracy, Rebellion, and Revolution.* , New York, NY: Ecco, 2019.

Rosalind S. Helderman, Matt Zapotosky, and Peter Finn. *The Mueller Report*. London, UK: Simon & Schuster, 2019.

Michael Isikoff and David Corn. *Russian Roulette: The Inside Story of Putin's War on America and the Election of Donald Trump*. New York, NY: Twelve, 2018.

Geoffrey M. Kabaservice. *Rule and Ruin: The Downfall of Moderation and the Destruction of the Republican Party, from Eisenhower to the Tea Party*. New York, NY: Oxford University Press, 2013.

David C. Johnston, *The Making of Donald Trump*. Richmond, Victoria, Australia: Hardie Grant Books, 2018.

Arthur C. Paulson. *Donald Trump and the Prospect for American Democracy: An Unprecedented President in an Age of Polarization*. Lanham, MD: Lexington Books,, 2018.

Philip Rucker and Carol Leonnig. *A Very Stable Genius: Donald J. Trump's Testing of America*. New York: Penguin , 2021.

Stuart Stevens. *It Was All a Lie: How the Republican Party Became Donald Trump* New York, NY: Alfred A. Knopf, 2020.

John K. White and Matthew R. Kerbel. *Party On!: Political Parties from Hamilton and Jefferson to Trump*. New York, NY: Routledge, 2018.

Rick Wilson. *Running against the Devil: A Republican Strategist's Plot to Save America from Trump—and the Democrats from Themselves*. New York, NY: Crown Forum, 2020.

Michael Wolff. *Fire and Fury*. New York, NY: Henry Holt and Co., 2018.

Index